*Issues in the Social Sciences*

# Gender in Flux

**In the Same Series**

*Crime: Fear or Fascination?*  edited by Anne Boran

# Gender in Flux

*Papers from a Conference held at
University College Chester,
November 2001*

Edited by Anne Boran and Bernadette Murphy

Chester Academic Press

First published 2004
by Chester Academic Press
Learning Resources
University College Chester
Parkgate Road
Chester CH1 4BJ

Printed and bound in the UK by the
Learning Resources Print Unit,
University College Chester
Cover designed by the
Learning Resources Graphics Team,
University College Chester

The introduction and editorial material ©University
College Chester, 2004
The individual chapters © the respective authors, 2004

All Rights Reserved
No part of this publication may be reproduced, stored in a retrieval system or transmitted in any form or by any means without the prior permission of the copyright owner, other than as permitted by current UK legislation or under the terms of a recognised copyright licensing scheme

Chapter 7 of this publication is a revised version of an article first published in *Capital and Class*, Vol. 75, Autumn 2001. It is included here with the agreement of the original publisher. Extracts from "An imperial nightmare", by Seumas Milne, quoted in Chapter 1, are included with the agreement of the copyright owner (© *The Guardian*, 2001).

A catalogue record for this book is available from the British Library

# CONTENTS

Contributors    vii

Foreword    xii

Acknowledgements    xv

Introduction    1
*Anne Boran and Bernadette Murphy*

1. Transforming Masculinities: Bodies, Power and Emotional Lives    13
   *Victor Seidler*

2. "Normals" and "Offenders": Classification Systems, Complacency and Critical Masculinities    35
   *Malcolm Cowburn*

3. "My Wife's Tongue Delivers More Punishing Blows Than Muhammed Ali's Fist": Bargaining Power in Nigerian Hausa Society    74
   *Fatima L. Adamu*

4. A Short History of Nature: Feminism and Transcendental Physiology    99
   *Jill Marsden*

5. Becoming Gendered: Feminist Beauty Ri(gh)tes    119
   *Karen Stevenson*

6.  "Cutting Up": Making Sense of  150
    Self-Harm
    *Mairead Owen*

7.  Caring or Not Caring: Academic  171
    Responses to Household and
    Labour Market Change
    *Jane Wheelock*

8.  Approaches to Gender and  192
    Development: Perspectives from
    Urban Mexico
    *Katie Willis*

# CONTRIBUTORS

**Professor Victor Jeleniewski Seidler** is Professor of Social Theory in the Department of Sociology, Goldsmiths College, University of London. He has written widely in the fields of social theory, ethics and gender. His more recent work includes *Recovering the Self: Morality and Social Theory* (Routledge, 1994), *Man Enough: Embodying Masculinities* (Sage, 1997) and *Shadows of the Shoah: Jewish Identity and Belonging* (Berg, 2000). More recently he has been working on the relationships between masculinities, global conflict and ethnicities.

**Dr Malcolm Cowburn** is Lecturer in Social Work and Social Policy at the University of Sheffield. His research interests are male sexual violence, men and masculinities, and life history research. His recent publications include: "Masking hegemonic masculinity: Reconstructing the paedophile as the dangerous stranger" (with Lena Dominelli), in *British Journal of Social Work*, 31, 2001, pp. 399-414; "Pornography and men's practices" (with Keith Pringle), in *Journal of Sexual Aggression*, 6, 2000, pp. 52-66; "Consultancy to group work programmes for adult male sex offenders: Some reflections on knowledge and processes", in *British Journal of Social Work*, 30, 2000, pp. 635-648; "A man's world: Gender issues in working with male sex offenders in prison", in *Howard Journal*, Vol. 37, No. 3, August 1998, pp. 234-251; and "The Black male sex offender in prison: Images and issues", in *Journal of Sexual Aggression*, Vol. 2, No. 2, 1996, pp. 122-142.

**Dr Fatima Adamu** is a Senior Lecturer in Sociology at Usmanu Danfodiyo University, Sokoto, Nigeria. Her research interests include the role of women as agents of change, the issue of gender and religion, and qualitative poverty assessment. Dr Adamu is currently engaged in two research projects: Islam and Women's Political Leadership in Northern Nigeria; and a Household Survey of Socio-Economic Dimensions of Poverty in Nigeria. Her publications include "A double-edged sword: Challenging women's oppression within Muslim society in Northern Nigeria", in *Gender and Development*, 7(1), March 1999, and "Gender myth about secluded women in Northern Nigeria", in *Gender perceptions and development in Africa*, edited by Mary Kolawole (Arrabon Academic Publishers, 1998). She has been a recipient of such awards as a British Chevening Scholarship and a Rockefeller Humanist Fellowship and she has also held positions in some professional organisations, such as Network for Gender and Women's Studies in Nigeria and the Association of African Women Scholars. She is also engaged in consultancy for some international funding and governmental agencies.

**Dr Jill Marsden** is Senior Lecturer in Philosophy at Bolton Institute of Higher Education. She began teaching at Bolton on completing her doctorate at the University of Essex in 1992. Between 1994-2000, she was responsible for running the Gender and Women's Studies Programme at Bolton. Her interests in gender issues particularly concern embodiment and the material conditions of thought and are pursued philosophically in a number of journal articles and edited collections.

**Dr Karen Stevenson** is Senior Lecturer in Sociology at Staffordshire University and manager of the Level 1 programme in Sociology and Crime, Deviance and Society. Her undergraduate teaching responsibilities draw on her interests in social and cultural theories of the body and in feminist and post-feminist issues, while her current research examines sex tourism, particularly in South-East Asia. She is a contributor to *The Collins Dictionary of Sociology (3rd ed., 2000)*, as well as to *Charlotte Perkins Gilman: Optimist Reformer* (J. Rudd & V. Gough, Eds.; University of Iowa Press, 1999); *The International Politics of Biotechnology: Exploring Global Futures* (A. Russell & J. Vogler, Eds.; Manchester University Press, 2000); and *Contested Bodies* (R. Holliday & J. Hassard, Eds.; Routledge, 2001. She has also published articles in the journal *Childright*.

**Dr Mairead Owen** is a freelance lecturer and researcher. She has recently retired as Senior Lecturer/Programme Leader in Sociology/Women's Studies at Liverpool John Moores University, where she is presently doing sessional lecturing in Equal Opportunities and in Media. She gained a First Class Honours Degree in Sociology from the Open University and went on to complete a Ph.D. on women and popular fiction at the University of Liverpool, under joint supervision from the English Department and the Department of Communications Studies. This very eclectic background characterises her research and teaching interests, which include feminism, media, equal opportunities, and the body. She has published and given papers on a variety of sociological, feminist and media topics, including the student experience, popular fiction, the body, equal opportunities, feminist pedagogy and feminist research.

**Professor Jane Wheelock** is Professor of Socio-Economics in the School of Geography, Politics and Sociology at the University of Newcastle upon Tyne. She has been researching the relationship between household lives and livelihoods since 1985. She is interested in the (gendered) inter-relations between the formal and the complementary economy and in the household as an institution. Much of her work has policy implications for work-life balance. Her books include: Vail, J., Wheelock, J., & Hill, M. (Eds.), *Insecure times: Living with insecurity in contemporary society* (Routledge, 1999); Wheelock, J., & Mariussen, A. (Eds.), *Households, work and economic change: A comparative institutional perspective* (Kluwer, 1997); and *Husbands at home: The domestic economy in a post-industrial society* (Routledge, 1990). She has three grown-up children.

**Dr Katie Willis** is Senior Lecturer in Geography at Royal Holloway, University of London. Her main research interests lie in the fields of gender and development, and trans-nationalism, gender and migration. She has conducted research in Mexico, Singapore, China and California. Her current research focuses on the gender and class impacts of health sector reform in Mexico, and on young people's identities in migrant communities in California. Her publications include *Gender and migration* (with Brenda Yeoh; Edward Elgar, 2000) and *Challenges and change in Middle America: Perspectives on development in Mexico, Central America and the Caribbean* (edited with Cathy McIlwaine; Pearson, 2002).

**Anne Boran (editor)** is Senior Lecturer and Undergraduate Programme Leader in the Department of Social and Communication Studies at University College Chester. Her teaching commitments are in the areas of the politics and economics of health, nutrition and health, the conference module – from which the inspiration for this series has come – and international development studies. Her fieldwork experience was in Brazil, where, as a community development worker, she was involved in shanty town projects involving living conditions, legal rights and, particularly, land rights. She has researched popular movements in Brazil and, inspired by this work overseas, has a particular interest in development studies. She also edited *Crime: Fear or fascination?*, the inaugural volume in this series.

**Dr Bernadette Murphy (editor)** has a First Class Honours Degree and a Ph.D. in Sociology from the University of Durham. She teaches Sociology, Research Methodologies and Gender and Health in the Department of Social and Communication Studies at University College Chester. She is currently writing a Health Studies textbook and a biography of her father. Her current research interests are eclectic and include work on the sociology of death, grief and mourning, adult education and research methodologies.

# FOREWORD

The term "gender" has become synonymous with a variety of complex meanings and representations that have been conceptualised by a wide range of academic writers. Such writers, be they philosophers, psychoanalysts or anthropologists, offer us fascinating insights into the construction of what is known as gender and they do so from a wide range of perspectives.

The binary categorisation of gender into a series of dichotomised opposites (based upon the premise of biological deterministic assumptions about gender) has, historically, been the subject of much debate. The feminist existentialist Beauvoir, for example, challenged both the secondary categorisation of women as inferior, and therefore women as "other", and the biological assumptions upon which this was based. In doing so, she rejected the call that one's sex was automatically one's gender. In a similar vein, the anthropologist Margaret Mead saw gender in terms of gendered behaviour that was constructed by and within cultural expectations. For her, gender reflected the norms and values of a given society, which, in turn, was attributed to biological differences. What was deemed masculine in one culture could be deemed feminine in another. For other theorists, it is biological sex that is itself shaped by cultural representations of gender and, developing this theme further, writers such as Delphy have contested the view that biological sex does not exist outside gender - as soon as we are born we are "gendered". Gender, in this context then, has no real meaning divorced from biological sex. Indeed, Delphy saw gender as a sex category, which is organised via a hierarchical division of labour and which

## Foreword

reinforces the pre-existing dichotomy between men and women, both in the private and public sphere.

What has become apparent in all disciplines is that studying gender offers theorists a vast and ever growing dimension of theoretical licence to deconstruct the term and show how it is represented in differing societies. This, in turn, allows for the location and exposure of the problematic nature of gendered assumptions in local and globalised market economies. In a postmodern world, this enables the proliferation of exciting new challenges in the field of gender. Current theorists have, for example, presented us with interesting debates, which have mainly focussed upon whether gender and sex as categories of meaning and discourse overlap. These fascinating themes have reinforced for us an important message – that gender is indeed in flux!

Building upon these important themes, this book, the second in the series *Issues in the Social Sciences*, expands and elaborates such arguments. *Gender in Flux* is based upon papers delivered at the annual conference organised for undergraduates at University College Chester and held in November 2001. Skilfully edited by its editors Anne Boran and Bernadette Murphy, it comprises a refreshing and informative collection of papers that reflect new approaches to the controversies that are prevalent in current debates about gender. In these chapters, the reader is presented with the opportunity to gain new insights into the construction of gender from both macro and micro viewpoints. This exciting compilation raises new questions about the perception and representation of gender, particularly masculinities, in contemporary global societies, together with analyses of the global influences that may alter such perceptions. In the post-September 11th world, this gives us food for thought. Furthermore, this collection asks us to examine existing ideas about nature and embodiment and the role nature plays in our performance of gender - a subject of much importance to gender theorists in the Judith Butler tradition. The renegotiations and realignment of gender roles, precipitated by capitalist driven market economies, need to be constantly reviewed in the light of current UK and EU work/life balance policies.

The writers in this volume are all well respected writers in the field of gender and gender studies and their contributions invite the reader to examine the above themes with flair and lively engagement. This book, *Gender in Flux*, emphasises the diversity of the term gender and alerts us to the dangers of becoming too complacent about the dynamics of this area of study. The changing nature and changing representations of gender are important areas of study and, as such, affect us all in our everyday lives. They should be constantly updated and revised in the light of the ever changing world that we all, whether male or female, inhabit.

*Chris Hepworth*
*Department of Health and Social Studies,*
*Bolton Institute of Higher Education*
*October 2003*

# ACKNOWLEDGEMENTS

Our thanks go to all those who have made this book possible. Sincere thanks to the volume's authors for their stimulating contributions to academic debate. Our thanks also go to Chris Hepworth for her astute and helpful comments.

A special note of appreciation to our students who chose such an interesting topic for the conference and who enthusiastically researched and debated key themes. The Department of Social and Communication Studies has, as ever, provided the kind of supportive environment for both academics and students that makes our annual conference possible and hence this publication.

We would like to acknowledge the contribution of staff in the Graphics Department, who patiently indulged our vague ideas and produced such interesting graphics for the theme. Lastly, our very sincere thanks and appreciation go to Peter Williams, Editorial Advisor of Chester Academic Press, who combines support and exacting standards in equal measure, for his invaluable advice and contribution to editing.

# INTRODUCTION

In this volume, three major themes are explored: masculinities, embodiment and culture, and the gender division of labour. These are important themes in a context in which it might have been supposed that debates about the nature of gender, and its implications for the workings of society, were exhausted. However, the European Council of Ministers is still having to produce more directives aimed at eliminating gender discrimination, levels of pay between men and women are still profoundly unequal, women lack weight in boardrooms and in the political sphere and men struggle to respond positively to the radical gender challenges presented to them by a world in flux. Theorists and policy makers are, therefore, continually provoked to revisit old debates and to raise new questions about what it is to be gendered.

The first three contributors, Victor Seidler, Malcolm Cowburn and Fatima Adamu, approach masculinities from different, but equally compelling, angles. Seidler deconstructs understandings of masculinity by examining the role of histories, both personal and collective, in shaping male identities. Cowburn uses masculinities to interrogate male sexual violence and Adamu demonstrates how dominant masculinity can be unmasked and undermined by female ingenuity.

In "Transforming Masculinities: Bodies, Power and Emotional Lives", Seidler argues that, from the recent felling of the Twin Towers to events played out in colonial times in other parts of the world, perceptions are shaped through the representations of the dominant powers. Framed in white, heterosexual terms, these representations shape the histories of those males involved in the collective projects of the imperial powers and those vanquished and dominated by them. Political rhetoric constructs an interpretation of events in terms of masculinities. It defines one set of male actors as "manly", brave and civilised and another as "unmanly", cowardly and uncivilised. The emotions and uncertainties generated under these conditions can, according to Seidler, transform fear of inadequacy into anger against the colonial "other". These global processes contribute to what he refers to as "a crisis of masculinity". However, globalisation also presents possibilities for the development of global identities that are detached from geographical locations. Postmodern society also provides possibilities for men to deconstruct and re-construct identities, perhaps on the basis of markers such as body image or patterns of consumption. Seidler argues that the fact that masculinities have been shaped by cultural expectations of male control over a dependent family – justified by the provision of subsistence – also helps to explain male crisis. Where this is still seen as part of male "role performance", various problems may emerge. For example, high levels of unemployment in developing countries may be correlated with high levels of violence against women, as in South Africa, or may drive men to seek recourse to the "certainties" offered by religious fundamentalism. The appeal of "tradition" offers men the security of a hierarchical order over which they can exercise some control in a world of change and uncertainty. In postmodern societies, young men are often unable to communicate, or recognise, the causes of their insecurity. Unable to confirm or to conform to secure masculinities, they may seek the solution to their problems in destructive behaviours of all kinds.

# Introduction

Malcolm Cowburn, in "'Normals' and 'Offenders': Classification Systems, Complacency and Critical Masculinities", focuses on the significance of masculinities for understanding violence in society, in this case sexual violence. He argues that the study of hegemonic masculinity, particularly, is a productive way to gain understanding of male sexual violence. Rather than simply focusing on offenders, as forensic scientific methods tend to do, Cowburn argues that a more fruitful sociological line of enquiry should focus on the general male population. Forensic science simply deflects attention from harmful male behaviours that are indulged in, and normalised by, society. For example, the perception of the male as heterosexual, dominant and "normally" aggressive serves to minimise the extent and impact of sexual violence, making it difficult to distinguish "normal" from "deviant" behaviour. Cowburn argues that sociological studies of masculinities, using self-reporting as a method of enquiry and focusing on male attitudes to sexual aggression in the general population, indicate that, far from being limited to a small number of deviant individuals, sexual violence is common in heterosexual relationships. It has to be suspected, therefore, that sexual offenders are located somewhere along the same continuum of male behaviours as are non-offenders or so-called "normals". Contrary to common perceptions, data examined by Cowburn suggests a low rate of re-conviction for convicted sex offenders and low numbers of offenders with previous convictions. Criminological data, however, suggest that the rate of sexual offending is on the increase, which could mean increased awareness and reporting and/or increased male aggression. Cowburn points to the former, claiming that feminist critiques have helped to unmask male hegemonic masculinity, leading perhaps to greater intolerance for aggressive behaviour towards females. Current "scientific" classificatory systems, therefore, while they may serve to reassure dominant groups in society that such behaviours are rare and performed by a small identifiable group, underestimate the effects of hegemonic masculinity on "normal" male sexual behaviour. This is something that society needs to engage with if violent male sexual behaviours are to be addressed.

In a delightful paper entitled, "My Wife's Tongue Delivers More Punishing Blows than Muhammed Ali's Fist: Bargaining Power in Nigerian Hausa Society", Fatima Adamu explores reactions to, and management of, dominant masculinity by women of (Muslim) Hausa society in Northern Nigeria. She begins with the Foucauldian notion that "where there is power, there is also counter-power", analysing ways in which women subvert structures of male domination so that, far from being victimised by them, they turn them to their advantage through challenge and negotiation. Adamu suggests that it is the contractual nature of marriage, in which financial maintenance by the husband is exchanged for seclusion (purdah) and obedience by wives, that enables this subversion. Wives use seclusion to their advantage, despite the mechanisms in place to support male domination, because the creation of separate spaces, involving mutual exclusion for both genders, creates the conditions for women to exercise greater autonomy in decision-making and to pursue activities that men cannot police. Adamu argues that seclusion, therefore, is a rational strategy for Hausa women to employ. It allows them to avoid the drudgery of farm work, including fuel and water collection, which is endured by many other African women. Seclusion allows a separate female economy to flourish, wherein children, old women and credit dealers provide links to the world outside. These allow women to sell goods that they make in their private

## Introduction

domain and to accumulate personal wealth, even by diverting resources from the household and therefore, indirectly, from their husbands. Seclusion enables networks of friendship and kinship to flourish, building solidarity among women, to their mutual benefit. Adamu argues that men are more dependent on marriage than women, since there is no stigma attached to divorce in Hausa society. Since gender relations are governed by contractual obligations, these can be used as bargaining chips. Failure to maintain the household adequately or any other breach of the marital contract, including sexual obligations, can be used to subvert male authority. When taken into the law courts or other public arenas, such power bargaining is a very useful strategic tool. It allows women to draw on the sympathy, arbitration and protection of others, in the knowledge that this causes men to lose face. Male power and domination is subverted in a non-violent, radically effective manner.

In their contributions to this volume, Jill Marsden, Karen Stevenson and Mairead Owen turn the focus of their analyses to the body and its relationship to gendered culture. Marsden focuses on historical approaches to understanding this relationship, Stevenson on the role of beauty/appearance in the gendering of the female body and Owen on relationships between female gender construction and the body, as they are signified by women who "cut", or deliberately mutilate themselves.

In "A Short History of Nature: Feminism and Transcendental Physiology", Jill Marsden provides a fascinating analysis of the history of feminist resistance to biological determinist accounts of women's bodies. She concludes that there is still a need to challenge the view that science is objective and gender neutral and that gender is predetermined by either biology or culture. This is necessary because some Second Wave feminists saw biology as the constraining influence on gender identity. Liberation from their bodies could, therefore, be provided for women through new and essentially controlling reproductive technologies. Marsden explores the limitations of this approach, given that culture tends to be coded as "male" and nature as "female". Since discourses throughout history have portrayed nature as something to be manipulated and shaped by culture, it is not likely that simply addressing biological difference will resolve the problem of gender identity. Marsden concludes that there is a gap in our knowledge and understanding of gender, which only a feminist physiology, which takes account of the realm of ideas, can fill. Simply possessing the natural capacity to be strong or to rape is not enough to make a rapist. The idea of rape has to be present in the mind of a man before it can be acted upon; which is not, however, to deny that ideas are social constructions. Rape is an excellent example of how Cartesian dualisms can be broken down if a feminist approach is applied to physiology. Neither physical nor psychological embodiment alone determines whether or not a man will become a rapist; it is patriarchal culture that does that. Consequently, Marsden argues, the challenge for a new philosophy of embodiment is to find ways of understanding nature that do not rely on patriarchal models.

In "Becoming Gendered: Feminist Beauty Ri(gh)tes", Karen Stevenson draws attention to the construction of appearance as an aspect of embodiment, which serves to construct "the stringent social hierarchy" that "separates the beautiful from the mundane" and both from "the drab, ugly and loathsome". Women are dependent on their appearance for social acceptance to an extent, she argues, that most men are not. Stevenson reviews feminist debate about the role of the construction of female beauty in

## Introduction

becoming gendered. First and Second Wave feminists, for example, explored the ways in which female bodies were gendered through (often painful) beauty rites, which subordinated "real" female identity in order to make women conform to male desires. They exposed the masquerade of feminine beauty and located it firmly in the cultural, rather than the natural, sphere. Beautiful women are made, not born. Second Wave feminists set about expressing "true" femininity, dressing for comfort and pleasure and challenging the male dominated beauty norms of the day. However, Stevenson argues, feminists experienced difficulties negotiating coherent feminist-liberated identities. They tended either to assume more "masculine" signifiers, thus placing themselves in opposition to feminine beauty norms, or to conform too closely to such norms, risking rejection as a betrayer of feminism. The assumption that some "real" femininity could be identified and represented underestimated, according to Stevenson, not only the cultural constraints of lived historical contexts, but also the ability of women to step beyond the acculured body. However, postmodern feminists have hailed the primacy of agency over structure. Women can shape the body and female identity as they choose. Gender is in flux, rather than fixed by physiological markers. With the body as a text to be inscribed through choices about appearance, consumption and lifestyle, being female can be a self-conscious formulation and re-formulation. The biological can also be moulded and shaped by surgery and drug treatments. Therefore, gender can be understood as an ongoing project and performance. Stevenson takes issue with such postmodern optimism. Self-beautification, she argues, cannot be reduced to processes of textual construction. There is no un-constructed "natural" beauty. Beauty possesses both physical and cultural dimensions.

Stevenson concludes that gender is perhaps not as much in flux as postmodernists would lead us to suppose. Since we are constrained in significant ways by the real situations and the material conditions in which we find ourselves (conditions such as class, race, ethnicity, location and history), we remain limited to some extent in what we may become.

In "Cutting: Making Sense of Self-Harm", Mairead Owen also addresses nature/body/self/identity relationships. She does so by examining the phenomenon of "cutting", by which some women harm their own bodies deliberately by attacking them with knives and razor blades. This behaviour has usually been understood, in earlier research conducted in mental institutions and prisons, as either mental illness or attention seeking on the part of the cutters. Owen's research, though limited in scale and scope, suggests that this is not so. Cutters, far from distancing, denigrating or despising the body because of mental illness or as a way of imposing control over it, communicated a sense of intense awareness of their embodiment as subjects. This condition of embodied subjectivity is, according to Owen, experienced particularly acutely as a reality by women, because they have to negotiate conditions such as menstruation, child bearing and menopause, which do not allow for distancing from the body in the ways that hegemonic masculinity, for example, does. Postmodern marginalisation of the physicality of embodiment and emphasis on the cultural construction of gender through performance does not quite capture the sense of the body experienced by cutters. Owen suggests that, for cutters, the body itself (because body and mind are one) is a means of directly communicating intolerable stress. The mutilation of the body enables the continued survival of the embodied subject until a more appropriate means of communication

## Introduction

can be found. This raises the question, however, of why some women need to communicate in this way and others do not.

The final theme of the book is that of the gendered division of labour. Jane Wheelock and Katie Willis provide excellent, complementary, papers on this theme; one focuses on the gender division of labour in the developed world and the other on gendered work and economic development in Mexico.

In "Caring or Not Caring: Academic Responses to Household and Labour Market Change", Jane Wheelock examines the changing dynamics of the gender division of labour, as capitalism re-shapes the lives of men and women through changes in the labour market. The focus of her research is the household and the ways in which formal waged employment interacts with unpaid domestic work. Wheelock argues that, as economic restructuring occurs, it will inevitably involve shifts between the market, the state and the household. She stresses, however, that it is the changing demands of the capitalist driven labour market that is promoting changes in gender roles, often referred to as "role reversal", and not any particular will of governments or people to contribute positively to these processes, by which gender can clearly be seen to be in flux. The major shift in relation to household livelihoods was, according to Wheelock, from that of family wage in an economic "regime of security" in the post-war era to that of family employment in an economic "regime of insecurity", produced by the freeing up of market forces in the post-Keynesian era. Demands for equality by women produced legislation, but changes in practice lagged behind it. The New Right agenda of the 1980s and 1990s gave greater power to markets and capital by making labour more "flexible". It also drove down wages. This "regime of insecurity" brought job insecurity, increasing polarisation of wealth and a shift from dependence on a family wage provided by a man to family employment involving men and women. Flexibility increased the use of female labour, often on a part-time basis. This provided some financial independence for women, but also demanded the continued maintenance of their domestic responsibilities and payment for child-care. A restructured economy facilitated continued male dependence, domestically, as well as male domination in the sphere of paid employment. It also added pressure to women's lives. The state demanded that the market deliver more child-care provision: if necessary, state-subsidised. This, policy makers believed, would allow women to enter the workplace on more equal terms. However, it simply increased the double burden on women. In addition, given the shortcomings of state-provided child-care facilities, children were not necessarily being cared for as well as they might have been in domestic contexts. Wheelock questions whether this model of family employment and state-regulated, market-delivered child-care is adequate. Complementary child-care, provided by grandparents, for example, might broaden options within households. She argues that theories such as those of Marx (in relation to the commodification of time) and Polanyi (in relation to the separation of the economic from the household spheres) need to be revisited in order to generate social policies that achieve a proper work/life balance.

In "Approaches to Gender and Development: Perspectives from Urban Mexico", Katie Willis examines the role of the gendered division of labour in providing solutions to the problems of equity and underdevelopment for men and women in a developing country. Gender relations in Mexico reflect typical inequalities across the world, but with the added burden of poverty and

## Introduction

economic under-development. In the late 1970s and 1980s, the country suffered a debt crisis. Neo-liberal reforms returned control to the markets and to competition, under the direction of International Monetary Fund/World Bank structural adjustment policies. These created high unemployment and Mexico, like Britain, came to depend on household-based strategies to survive economically. Intensification of labour, according to Willis, pushed women in increasing numbers into working in the informal sector, where reproductive tasks could be combined with flexible work. Multinational companies provided formal employment on the Mexican border. This was particularly reliant on female labour. However, men were employed in supervisory jobs, even when the majority of the workers on the shop floor were women. Whether or not allowing women into the labour force leads to empowerment (an approach much lauded in Development Studies) is open to question. Much evidence suggests that women end up working a double day: taking part in paid employment while continuing with their domestic labour. This does not necessarily empower women, but it certainly overburdens them. Willis concludes that, if women are to be empowered through the implementation of development policies, those policies must pay attention to gender relationships and not treat the economic needs of women as if they are simply add-ons. Existing male-dominated working practices do not meet the economic needs of women. Consequently, Willis argues, as have other authors in this volume in relation to different aspects of gender relations, masculinities need to be deconstructed in ways that allow for positive responses to changes in the labour market and the household division labour, if development policies are to succeed.

*Gender in Flux* is the second volume in the *Issues in the Social Sciences Series,* based on papers, aimed principally at undergraduate students, delivered during the Department of Social and Communication Studies' Annual Conference at University College Chester in 1991. Participants in the Conference were invited to explore the ways in which gender relationships in contemporary societies could be understood to be changing and, therefore, to be in flux. The result was a fascinatingly diverse range of interpretations of that theme and a lively and intellectually stimulating debate, which is reproduced in this book. All of the contributors to this volume advance our knowledge about the ways in which gender can be understood to be in flux. They draw on the long dynamic history of feminists' engagement with the problematic nature of gender and gender relations. However, they also engage critically with the work of more recent theorists of masculinities in deconstructing, and challenging, how masculinities continue to be shaped by society, in ways that are detrimental to stable gender relations and to society itself.

# 1

# TRANSFORMING MASCULINITIES: BODIES, POWER AND EMOTIONAL LIVES

## Victor Seidler

When I first agreed to do this paper[1], which was in the summer, I had a pretty good idea of what I wanted to say about transforming masculinities, but September 11th 2001 and the build-up to the war in Afghanistan seems to have changed so many things. In so many ways, the situation that we are living through is about conflicting masculinities. When Bush says, "You are either with us or against us", and when this is echoed by Blair, there is no middle ground. There is no space for thought. Ambivalence and even doubt seems to show a lack of resolve and so a lack of masculinity.

The war and the preparation for the war reflected certain notions about men and masculinity that I wanted to be able to talk about, because it is part of all our experience. It has also been part of the lives of my students. Young men who are in London and who see themselves as quite confirmed in their masculinity are feeling uneasy about taking the tube (the underground) and one student is doing a project, interviewing men about the uncertainties and the fears that have come to the surface, which have led to the young men making only

---

[1] This paper was originally given as a lecture to the Gender in Flux Conference, just over two months after the events of September 11th 2001. I would like to express my appreciation to the students and staff who worked so hard to produce a warm and stimulating atmosphere. I thank Anne Boran, Bernadette Murphy and Peter Williams for the work they did to transform a verbal presentation to written form.

necessary journeys. Another young Muslim student is working on her dissertation, which is about the violence she has personally experienced since September 11th on the streets of East London and her experience of being spat at on the tube by two 11-year-olds, who in some ways could not have understood what they were doing.

So I will talk about where we are now, but I also have to say something about where we have come from historically, to be in this situation now. The writing that I did especially for today's paper was done in the shadows of September 11th, so it is indirect and it works towards the issues of the Conference. So much is in flux, not only our gender identities, and if we are to understand those identities we have to understand where we have come from. I am going to split my paper into four sections.

*Echoes*

In the first part I am going to talk about echoes: echoes of a past that is somehow still here. A recent (2001) article in the *Guardian* by Seumus Milne argued, "the new [Anglo-American] appetite for intervention will only increase the likelihood of anti-Western terror". He argued, and this struck a chord with me, that "Britain has yet to come to terms with its imperial record. A fog of cultural amnesia about the nation's recent colonial past pervades the debate about its role in the world today". He recalls that, "in the run-up to the millennium", the twentieth century that we have just left was remembered as "a century of bloodshed and tyranny, with the Nazi genocide and Stalinist terror regularly paired as the emblematic twin horrors of the period". These were the two defining experiences of the twentieth century.

He also noted, "the modern school history curriculum reflects a similar perspective". So, think about the kind of histories we learnt at school and the kind of assumptions about gender, particularly about men and masculinity, which we internalised through those particular histories. As Milne says,

> ... when it comes to the role of colonialism and its aftermath, British reactions are usually cloaked in either embarrassment or retrospective pride about a legacy of railways and "good governance". There is precious little acknowledgement of the relentless and bloody repression that maintained a quarter of the world's population under British rule until barely half a century ago. (Milne, 2001, p. 19)

Moreover, phenomena such as the slave trade in Liverpool have to be understood in order to understand the wealth of a city like Chester and the conditions in which you are doing your own thinking. But often those histories have barely been scratched at. We pass them over, yet those histories shape not only a sense of ourselves as men and as women, but also our gendered identities.

I can recall growing up in North West London in the 1950s in the shadows of the Empire. We grew up in school to feel proud of the pink areas in our atlases that represented the Empire; that shows you how things have changed in our generation. There was a sense of pride that helped shape our masculinities and made us, as children of refugees from Nazi rule in Europe, which was my own history, very much want to belong. Since we were born in England, we felt that we, at least, could "become English", even if our parents - my parents came from Vienna and from Warsaw - were in some ways bound to remain foreign.

We learnt that we had to forget where we had come from in order to feel that we could belong here. I can also recall the news when I was growing up, which was often about "terrorists" who were fighting against colonial rule. We constantly heard about the terrible violence (and this sounds very distant, but it certainly shaped my own masculinity) perpetrated by the Mau Mau in Kenya as an attack by the "primitive" on the "civilised" and "ethical" intentions of British rulers, who were only there to bring progress and civilisation. This was still heard of as "the White man's burden", as if the Empire had everything to give and nothing to gain for itself. It was the project of a dominant, White, heterosexual masculinity, in which young men were trained to take their part in that imperial project.

The Empire was represented as possessing a selfless and altruistic devotion to the other peoples, who constantly failed to appreciate what was being done for them. The colonised were thus identified with children, who never appreciate what their parents are doing for them. As Milne (2001) reminders us,

> It is less than 50 years since British soldiers were paid 5 shillings for each Kenyan they killed, nailed the limbs of Mau Mau fighters to crossroad posts and had themselves photographed with the severed heads of Malayan guerrillas. But - as with other forms of Colonial power, such as France and Belgium - there has been no public settling of accounts. No pressure for Colonial reparations or for old men to

be tried for atrocities carried out under the Union flag. (Milne, 2001, p. 19)

This was the commonsense that we grew up with in my generation. It has, in some ways, been forgotten already, erased in the generations that have grown up since. Bringing back some of these echoes not only makes us feel our age, my age as an older man, for example, but also gives us a sense of how radically the world has changed. What we have learnt to forget is how hard it is to understand the historical constructions of our own masculinities.

Young men were trained to play their part in the project of Empire and it left generations of working class and middle class men with a particular sense of white supremacy that could somehow cut across the antagonisms of class. Some of those antagonisms recently broke open in the North of England, in Oldham and other cities, where exactly the kind of historical conditions that I am mentioning need to be reflected upon in order to understand the violent events of the summer.

As with the Empire, so also the First and Second World Wars were testing grounds for masculinities; ways of proving that you were man enough. How did you know that you were a "real" man if you had not fought, because traditionally masculinities were identified with proving that you had fought in the War and so having put your male identity beyond threat? As I argued in *Rediscovering Masculinity* (1989) and later in *Man Enough* (1997), one of the difficulties with masculinity is the idea that it is something you constantly have to be ready to defend. If someone is offensive to you, you have to be prepared to say: "I'll see you outside after the lecture".

Masculinity is something that can never be assumed in the West. It is something that you need always to be ready to defend and certain emotions and feelings regarded as signs of weakness become threats to that masculinity, particularly in the context of September 11th and the notion of fear. What was the fear that people felt? Could that fear be acknowledged and named?

Often young women can acknowledge fear, because it is not taken to be a threat to their feminine identities, but with men it is different; that fear is taken to be a threat to a male identify, so that fear is never really acknowledged.

Just think for a minute or two about the questions: "How did I learn fear?"; "Is fear gendered?". Certain emotions and feelings are gendered and shaped in a particular way in relationships, and fear is a very good example, because young men in particular learn that fear is something that does not belong to masculinity. To feel fear can give the appearance of weakness and to be a weak man is, in terms of heterosexual masculinity, in some ways not to be a man at all. So fear, like loneliness, like isolation, is something that we do not want to have to recognise and so we do not, in some way, become conscious or aware of that fear or of that vulnerability. Learning as men to control our emotions can work to estrange us, so that often we just do not know what we are feeling or feel that we lack a language with which to express them.

As soon as fear begins to emerge, we put it aside or it becomes transformed and (Freud's psychoanalysis helps us think about this) it gets transformed into anger. So, rather than being able to feel or acknowledge the fear before it is named, it becomes anger against the other and often is the source of male violence towards women. It is the difficulty of men acknowledging and coming to terms with the complexity of their own emotional lives that turns anger into violence in relationships with women.

In this context, it reflects the history that I am trying to talk about. The colonial other becomes the place or the space in which violence, institutional violence in the context of war, comes to be worked out. This is why issues of war have in the West traditionally been tied up with questions of men and masculinity. We prove that we are "man enough" and show that we can prevail and have the moral fibre not to give in, not to sacrifice our principles before the long battle for victory. Such rhetoric possibly sounds old-fashioned, but it was the rhetoric that Blair recently invoked to make sure that people did not weaken in their resolve to support the bombing of Afghanistan. If women might be expected to "weaken", then men would be there to steady nerves, to see things through.

We seem to be living in a different, in some ways more dangerous, world after September 11th and, unless we reflect carefully about how we came to be here, things could get even more uncertain and dangerous, as has been shown in the second Iraq War. Bush was quick to call the perpetrators of the attacks on the twin towers in New York, "mindless cowards"; again, rhetoric in relation to masculinity that we might not have even heard, because it already resonated with our own preconceptions. Although Bush must have recognised the careful planning and the risks individuals were taking with their lives, his rhetoric still suggested that, while it showed "manly" courage to sacrifice your life for your country, it was "evil fanaticism" that was "unmanly" when it led to such horrendous attacks on civilian lives.

This was to be set against the heroic working class masculinities that were well demonstrated by the New York Fire Department who, quite rightly, became the heroes of the hour.

## Prophecies

Blair is the first post-war prime minister, the first to be born after the Second World War, so he never got the chance to test his masculinity in the realities of war; which may be is why he " ... has led Britain into four wars in four years - against Iraq, Yugoslavia, Sierra Leonean rebels and now Afghanistan. So far, British and US casualties have been negligible. But the likely costs are now rising" (Milne, 2001). As Milne further reminds us,

> When British troops slaughtered the followers of the Mahdi in Sudan or the Muslims of northern Nigeria a century ago, the fighting was far from home and the colonial forces had overwhelming technological superiority. "Whatever happens", wrote Hilaire Belloc, "we have got the Maxim gun and they have not". Retaliations for colonial atrocities in the metropolitan heartland - such as the attempted assassination in London of General Dyer, the man who ordered the 1919 Amritsar massacre - were rare. Now all that has changed. Since September 11th, we have discovered that the empire can strike back. (Milne, 2001, p. 19)

This might be part of the story, but Milne's account itself needs to be put into a broader context of changes that have taken place. One of the most significant changes wrought by globalisation and the decline of traditional industries in different parts of the world is the absence of work, not only in Muslim countries, but also across the Third World (the South). In particular, there is an absence of work for a growing population of young men. This is also very clear in South Africa and other areas, where we are seeing increases in violence, linked to young men who have no employment and who can no longer hope to sustain their male identities as breadwinners or providers. We need to think about how the attraction to religious fundamentalism is related to crises in traditional masculinities.

In traditional societies, in which you need an income in order to get married and you need to get married in order to have sexual relations, this has worked to exclude many young men from sexual relations. It has also produced a pervasive anger directed at the West, which is perceived as having undermined local industries that might have otherwise provided employment opportunities. Through globalisation, the terms of which have largely been set by Western corporations, the work that has been available in some areas of the world, such as Mexico, is often for women; for example, producing goods for Nike. With women having a source of income, this can serve to undermine and destabilise traditional gender relations. As those relations become unstable, young men can feel fear about how they are to sustain their traditional male identities and that fear often gets translated into anger, into hitting out, into violence.

Religious movements, for instance, can within this context seem to reinstate traditional masculinities and give ways of affirming male identities that would otherwise be threatened. In the United States, we have had Christian fundamentalist movements like the Promise Keepers, which have re-inscribed traditional masculinities, with men returning to their authority figure roles as fathers in the home and woman having to accept the so-called leadership or authority of men. So in the West, partly in response to feminism, we have had men's rights movements that have seen feminism as in some way the enemy, because feminism was seen as questioning and challenging traditional visions of patriarchal authority; the notion of "who wears the trousers". The underlying idea is that, if there is not a single person in the family who is in authority, there has to be chaos. That vision of a single authority is re-inscribed within religious traditions in the West, but we are seeing it in religious traditions in the East too. So, when people talk about a conflict between different civilisations, which I think is a dangerous way of framing it, it is often religious movements that have been seen as reinstating man's traditional authority.

It also attracts men, by giving them a sense of a superior status in an uncertain globalised world. In Britain, there is also an appeal to young Muslims, who might otherwise feel marginalized and unable to find work, even though they have formal school qualifications. They experience discrimination in the labour market and they are not prepared to accept the second-class status of being different that they experience with their parents. Rather, young men feel entitled to belong, but they feel that, as British Muslim men, they are not really accepted. They might have tried, but felt as if they had been thrown back. This again can promote the appeal of a certain kind of religious fundamentalism. But, when we talk about gender in flux, it is also the global media and the Internet that have made globalised identities available to people in different local areas. Within virtual space, young people can define themselves in different ways.

I was visiting Gothenburg in Sweden, doing some work, when I was struck by how the migrant community in that area (often young, South American men, who had come from Chile, but also migrants who had come from Africa), who were living on the outskirts of the city of Gothenburg, identified themselves; not in terms of wanting to become Swedish, not in terms of wanting to become "like everyone else", but through an identity with Hip-Hop and the Hip-Hop nation. Even if Gothenburg is where they live, it does not mean that this is where they belong. Rather, and I was very struck by this, they connected their local space to the global identity of Hip-Hop; and it was through the Internet that they felt more connected with what was happening in Los Angeles, in terms of the music that identified their masculinities, than they did with what was happening in Sweden. So this was another response to a globalisation that has meant the movement of populations across different nation states and the creation of different kinds of masculinity, so that these options have become available through global media.

Within a more multicultural Britain, there is less pressure upon young people from migrant cultures to feel that they need to assimilate into a dominate culture; to feel that they have to fulfil the dream of modernity (which was very much the experience of my own upbringing), which allows the person defined as "different" or "other" to become like the majority. The centre no longer has the kind of hold that it did when I was growing up in the 1950s, when we felt that we should pay the price of subordinating our ethnic, religious or spiritual identities in order to belong, in order to "become English". Now there is a pluralisation of diverse British identities and of diverse masculinities; different ways in which you can imagine yourself as Black British or British Asian or British Muslim, though whether or not "British" can be said to "come first" might indicate different relationships and a different positioning in relation to a colonial past. But it means that histories no longer have to be forgotten in order that you can become like everybody else. Rather, you expect your history to be visible and recognised, as part of being respected for who you are. To know who you are, and this is true of all of us in different ways, depends upon where you have come from.

*Histories*

I was struck recently, in relation to the incidents in Oldham and other parts of the North of England, that the British National Party had renamed one of its magazines *Identity*. I was also struck by the way in which this Fascist movement was now thinking of itself and describing its journal as a journal of identity, for this involved coming to terms with a multicultural vision of diverse masculinities, which meant that others could be acknowledged as friends, but not as family. The "others" are still different; they have a different identify. The British National Party was claiming a vision of Whiteness and White masculinities and setting it as an "ethnic identity" amongst others.

As Les Back (1994) and others have stressed, this is a misleading strategy. It is helpful to think of diverse masculinities, in which White masculinity, along with Black and Asian masculinities, can be thought of as moving away from a singular notion of masculinity towards a plural vision of different masculinities. For Back, this is a misleading strategy, because it refuses to acknowledge the power and privilege that has traditionally gone along with Whiteness within the project of British colonialism. Postmodern thinkers, on the other hand, do not just want to set another seat at the table; rather they are wary of any fixed notion of masculinity or ethnic identity or of communities. They want to stress that identities are open and fluid and that gender is always in flux and hybrid, always drawing upon a whole variety of different influences. They can bring together different influences and celebrate their connections to diverse and pluralistic inheritances, rather than having to choose a single ethnicity whose boundaries have to be policed as carefully as those of a White, young, working-class man.

Arguments in relation to "race" and ethnicities partly echo a similar discussion that has been taking place in work about masculinities, particularly as in the work of Connell (1987, 1995), where masculinities have been defined exclusively in terms of male power and privilege. So often, the reason that a lot of younger men growing up in a supposedly more equal gender world do not want to have much to do with gender is because they do not experience themselves as powerful and privileged, although the theoretical work often only sees masculinity in terms of power and privilege. The issue then was how masculinity could be deconstructed, particularly in a kind of anti-sexist men's politics, but also in certain kinds of post-structural work, because masculinity and men were seen to be the problem.

Redefining masculinities could in no way be recognised as part of the solution. When I wrote my first book in the mid-1980s, I called it *Rediscovering Masculinity* and I did that provocatively, because people said that masculinity is everywhere and so it does not have to be rediscovered. What I was trying to argue is that, even though masculinity in some ways is everywhere, it is an important step, particularly for men, to begin to recognise our experience as gendered. When we look in the mirror in the morning, we often only see a person, because masculinity is taken to be universal. It has become the marker of a universal identity, so it takes time for men to say, "I am not just a human being, a person, I am also a man and the way that I feel and think about myself has been shaped by my conditioning, my experiences, and the way that I have been treated as a man within the context of family and school".

Let me just give you an example. If something has happened at home, where do young men and women look for support? What does support mean to them and, if there was either a divorce or separation at home or if somebody had died, would there be significant gender differences in the patterns of support at school? Would you, as a young person, talk to other young women, would you talk to young men or would you keep it to yourself?

Now some of the research shows why gender is so powerful - because potentially it can take us from thinking in terms of our own individual personal experience to questions of larger structures of power. If you take notions of support, research shows that young women more easily ask for or will talk and draw support, because support is somehow less threatening to feminine identity. For young men, it can be difficult, for example, to say that they feel upset about what happened last night, because support is linked to having emotional needs; and the idea of acknowledging emotional needs is a form of being dependent and is threatening both to heterosexual and gay identities, but often more to heterosexual masculinities, because having emotional needs is already seen as a threat to heterosexual ideas of being male. Men learn to think that they have to be independent and independence is thought about in terms of being self-sufficient; and being self-sufficient means, "I can cope with my life on my own, thank you very much". What becomes important is some notion of "front", of not "losing face", but presenting a "front" to other men and other women in which men are seen as capable, or at least in control of their lives, because there is a very powerful identification between masculinity and self-control and with the idea of needing to be in control of your emotional life.

This is very important, because it is often used against men. If, for instance, a firm is moving to a different place and the family of one of its male employees, his partner and the children, say, "We don't want to move. We have got all our friends in Chester, we don't want to move to Aberdeen". It can be very difficult, in terms of masculinity, to say, "Well, my family refuses to move", because it would seem that you do not have control of the traditional family unit and, if you do not control your family, how can you be expected to control the rest of your life? So, men might at the moment often have "more equal" relations at home, but in relationships with the corporate sector feel forced in some way to present themselves quite traditionally, as being in control of their families.

This notion of being in control can also block communication between fathers and sons and daughters. Often, that communication does not exist, or is limited, because it has become difficult for men to acknowledge their own emotional needs or a sense of emotional support. Rather men grow up in diverse class and ethnic backgrounds often feeling that they "should" be able to deal with their emotional problems on their own.

To define masculinity exclusively in terms of relationships of power is as misleading as to think of "Whiteness" simply as a notion that needs to be deconstructed. It has taken time for men, in particular, to recognise our experience as gendered, as masculine and it is something that often takes time. It involves thinking about our experience in radically different ways in order to begin to think and conceptualise experience in quite different terms, through being able to name it as masculine. But often, as men, we have done that naming very quickly and we have been happy to move from thinking about masculinity to thinking about gender, so assuming a false parallelism with feminist work, which has been engaged in these questions for over twenty years.

However, it might have been important for different generations of men to have considered more deeply what it means to be "masculine" and how their male identities have been shaped. I want to raise some questions about this and its relationship with notions of gender flux.

*Uncertainties*

Often, today, young men are unsure of who they are and what they want to become. Many young women take equality with young men for granted, whilst assuming that feminism either belongs to an earlier generation or that they know all about it, as if whatever it had to offer has somehow been assimilated. So, young women often feel distant from feminism, as if it were something that had to do with their mother's generation and as if the claim to equality means that feminism is somehow past and unnecessary.

There is a conflict between generations, between different generations of women as well as between different generations of men; but young men are often less concerned with questions about feminism. They can ask about men and masculinity and want to know about their experience as men, without having to work out their relationship to feminism. This is quite unlike the experience of my generation, which in the 1970s was always engaged in trying to work out its relationship with feminism; and that, I think, in many ways produced some of the problems we are faced with now.

An example of this conflict between generations is in the art world. The artist Tracey Emin draws on her own personal history, her experiences of her relationships and of her abortions. These become part of her artwork. She recognises how these experiences, her own past, continue to echo in her thinking in a way that feminism has opened up. So, it is only because of feminist work that she could do the artwork that she does. Although she feels indebted to her feminist teachers, she thinks that feminism is in some way not for her, because the teachers all dressed in dungarees and were not concerned with "making it" or being successful in their careers.

They were not concerned with thin bodies, with clothes or with hedonism in the same way as young women of this generation, who feel that they can drink any guy they are out with under the table. So there is a cultural shift towards hedonism and a culture of laddism or laddishness, towards a different kind of masculinity and a different kind of femininity. In some ways, this has to do with different visions and pleasures, but also with a cynicism that refuses to take the world seriously and feels ironic towards an earlier generation. The first and second waves of feminism are deemed too serious, not concerned enough with fun.

For young men, there are also changes in terms of a new body culture that has to do with the "hard body". For example, the idea that working out in the gym shows the moral qualities of self-control. So, we again have the notion of masculinity and control, but it is now shaped through a different relationship: to image, to consumer culture, to clothes. For, with the decline of traditional modes of affirming masculinities, such as the scarcity (with globalisation) of the traditional work that used to define male identities, the body has become a site that crosses over the boundaries of class, at least for those who can afford to go to the gym. Money has now become the divider, marking success through the car you can afford to drive and the holidays you can afford to take.

But there are also new fears, which an older generation of men did not know about in the same way. For there is an anxiety about men's bodies, about "being fat", about young men wondering if they are fat and therefore fears about eating. So conditions like anorexia, identified twenty years ago, although still much more linked to women, are now increasingly being seen in relation to young men and masculinities. There is also the anxiety to be current, to be "cool", to be "wicked". There are fears that life has somehow passed you by, that you are not with the international youth styles, that there is a pluralisation of styles, that there are some bands you just do not listen to. So, there are indicators of gender in flux defining current masculinities that need to be identified and explored.

As I have said, there is a fear of fat as young men, like young women, also see themselves through the images of consumer culture and there is a need for control, which can be worked out through the idea of controlling the body. But there is still unease when it comes to personal life and emotional life; a fear of dependency, with men feeling, in new and often in more intense ways, which they need to be in control. But often, as our thinking has shown, this means that men can still find it hard to reach out to others emotionally; can still feel that it is a sign of weakness to need support from others; that to have emotional needs reflects a threat to male identities.

Within a postmodern culture, there are uncertainties that create new anxieties, for you can feel that you should already know the answers to problems and that, if you have to ask others, you are giving them the opportunity to put you down. So men are always in fear of "losing face" in front of other men, because, if their vulnerability is made visible, there is a fear that it will be used against them.

At school, there is now a more intense fear of failure, which leads pupils to feel that it is better not to try, not to put in effort, because then they cannot "really" have failed.

So, all the questions about boys' underachievement at school link to a reframing of masculinity within a different cultural setting. Within the increasingly competitive atmosphere in schools, because of the ways that schools are now graded and tested, young men are being told that they have been out-performed academically by women. It is easy for men to compensate by assuming a front of, "It makes no difference to me" and this front becomes increasingly hard and makes it increasingly hard to make contact. But, as a front is presented to the outside world, so there is often a division or split within that emotional interior.

Men's inner feelings are often very different from what they can express outside. Even if there is a new emotional fluency for some young men and an easing of boundaries between gay and straight men, there is also a fear of sharing the uncertainty; the loneliness and depression that young men still fear they have to carry on their own. Tragically, it is often easier for young men to commit suicide than to reach out to friends and others for help. They do not want to bother others or lean on them, because there is still a pervasive sense within diverse masculinities that men should be able to make it on their own; that if life confronts them with problems, they should be able to solve them on their own. This shows itself at an early age at school. Where, as a young man, would you ask for support? What kind of histories did we learn that shaped and reshaped our visions of masculinity for our particular generation?

Often, if parents divorce or a relative dies, girls will more easily reach out, but boys will feel the pain just as much, but it is easier to pretend that things are OK and that you do not really need the support of others, for needing support somehow still threatens the male identities that young men feel they need to perform. But, in "gender as performance" mode, they often use drink and drugs so as not to feel what is going on. To perform can also mean to escape, through the rituals of substance abuse and those of a firmly controlled world, from one that feels increasingly out of control.

As men and women, we live in a different world from our parents or grandparents. Much more information is available to us, but often we can feel more uneasy about who we want to be and how we want to be in relationships with others. There are no longer the models that existed in previous generations, in which you could confirm or conform to traditional models. There are new anxieties, new fears and new definitions of what it means for men and women in heterosexual relationships and men in gay relationships to be open, honest and communicative with each other. But often this means sharing fears, the kind of fears that have emerged since September 11th and opening communication in families, when traditionally there was often a withdrawn silence when we needed to communicate, because we felt that these were things that we could not do.

*References*

Back, L. (1994). *New ethnicities and urban culture: Racism and multiculturalism in young lives.* London: UCL Press.

Connell, R. W. (1987). *Gender and power: Society, the person and sexual politics.* Cambridge: Polity Press.

Connell, R. W. (1995). *Masculinities.* Cambridge: Polity Press.

Milne, S. (2001, November 8). An imperial nightmare. *The Guardian*, p. 19.

Seidler, V. J. (1989). *Rediscovering masculinity: Reason, language and sexuality.* London: Routledge.

Seidler, V. J. (1997). *Man enough: Embodying masculinities.* London: Sage.

*Additional Reading*

Brittan, A. (1989). *Masculinity and power.* Oxford: Basil Blackwell.

Chapman, R., & Rutherford, J. (Eds.) (1988). *Male order: Unwrapping masculinity.* London: Lawrence & Wishart.

Cockburn, C. (1998). *The space between us: Negotiating gender and national identities in conflict.* London: Zed Books.

Enloe, C. (1993). *The morning after: Sexual politics at the end of the Cold War.* Berkeley: University of California Press.

Frosh, S., Phoenix, A., & Pattman, R. (2002). *Young masculinities: Understanding boys in contemporary society.* Basingstoke: Palgrave.

Gray, J. G. (1998). *The warriors: Reflections on men in battle.* Lincoln: University of Nebraska Press. (Original work published 1959).

Hedges, C. (2002). *War is a force that gives us meaning.* New York: Public Affairs.

Ignatieff, M. (1997). *The warrior's honor: Ethnic war and the modern conscience.* New York: Metropolitan Books.

Mac an Ghaill, M. (1994). *The making of men: Masculinities, sexualities and schooling.* Buckingham: Open University Press.

Seidler, V. J. (1991). *Recreating sexual politics: Men, feminism and politics.* London: Routledge.

Seidler, V. J. (1994). *Unreasonable men: Masculinity and social theory.* London: Routledge.

Thorne, B. (1993). *Gender play: Girls and boys in school.* Buckingham: Open University Press.

Walkerdine, V. (1997). *Daddy's girl: Young girls and popular culture.* Basingstoke: Macmillan.

# 2

# "NORMALS" AND "OFFENDERS": CLASSIFICATION SYSTEMS, COMPLACENCY AND CRITICAL MASCULINITIES

## Malcolm Cowburn

*Introduction*

The aim of this chapter is to suggest that forensic perspectives on male sexual violence are inadequate to address issues of community safety, because they fail to address masculinities. By "forensic" perspectives, I am referring particularly to the endeavours of clinical psychology, and to a lesser extent psychiatry, to understand sexual violence within a "natural science paradigm" that largely ignores the social context of sexual violence.

The title for this chapter was prompted by the following quotation from Richard Laws in a paper entitled "How dangerous are rapists to children?" When reviewing the data relating to male sexual response with accounts of coercive sexual behaviour in both self-report surveys and physiological assessments (known as "phallometric testing"), Laws (1994, p. 8) was unable to distinguish, clearly and consistently, the convicted rapist from the so-called "normal" male. He notes:

> ... more alarming, perhaps, are the findings from self-reports and phallometric testing of so-called normal males. Here we find

patterns of behaviour and sexual response that are strikingly similar to those of sexual offenders, suggesting considerable overlap in their developmental histories. Those who proceed to become adult sex offenders apparently fail to develop the inhibitions that constrain normals. For their part, normals appear to harbour many of the same feelings, have the same fantasies, but fail to act upon them.

The bi-polar division ("normals" and "sex offenders") outlined by Laws troubles me for a number of reasons. It is noteworthy that Laws's non-sex offending category is identified as "normals" – clearly a group without a gender, which conforms to some unidentified, but absolute, standard of behaviour. It is equally important to note that Laws describes sex offenders and normals in a way that ignores their sex. The literature that he reviewed concerned the attitudes and behaviours of *men* – whether or not they were convicted of a sexual offence.

The forensic discourse about sex offenders is epistemologically rooted in a positivist, natural science approach to "scientific" enquiry. In this chapter, I will consider the gendered nature of this scientific discourse and how it has shaped understandings of male heterosexuality and the nature of the sex offence. In this context, I will review current sex offender classification systems. One aspect of discourse in this area is to minimise understanding of the extent and nature of sexual violence. To counteract this picture, I refer to three particular bodies of literature – recidivism studies, prevalence studies and self-report studies. Recidivism studies have examined the patterns of reconviction –

including the nature of the offence and the length of time before a fresh offence is committed – of a variety of sex offender populations. A popular assumption relating to sex offenders is that they are a small group with a high rate of reconviction; this is manifestly not the case. Prevalence studies provide a picture of the general extent of sexual violence in society and self-report studies, by men who have not been convicted of sexual offences, provide a picture of the proportion of men who would, in certain circumstances, commit acts of sexual aggression. I conclude the paper by suggesting that sex offender classification systems do not contribute to a social understanding of male sexual violence, because they focus exclusively on convicted men and, in the aetiology of sex offending underlying them, gender is irrelevant. I suggest that an examination of the forms of masculinities, particularly hegemonic masculinity, may provide a more productive key to understanding and possibly reducing the prevalence of sexual violence.

Harding (1991, p. 288-295) has written of "traitorous identities", by which she refers to the process whereby people with culturally dominant identities (e.g. "White" or "male" or "heterosexual") are able to critique the dominance of their group with insight gained from familiarity with the perspectives of people in oppressed groups. This paper is written from a pro-feminist perspective; it is the perspective of a man who is critical of unexamined male hegemonic assumptions about epistemology and knowledge relating to sexual violence. I am also concerned that, without engaging in this scrutiny and developing alternative ways of speaking about and responding to male sexual violence, the classification and treatment of convicted sex offenders will merely continue to obscure a much wider issue – harmful male behaviours.

## *The Gendered Nature of Scientific Discourse*

In a useful paper concerning the invisibility of male theorists in social theory, Hearn (1998) has pointed out that what often stands as "objective" social science is, in effect, the world-view of a socially and economically dominant group of men. This group asserts its hegemonic power through "scientific" discourse, in which their world-view masquerades as the "objective truth". Connell (1995, p. 77) has described "hegemonic masculinity" as " ... the configuration of gender practice which embodies the currently accepted answer to the problem of the legitimacy of patriarchy, which guarantees (or is taken to guarantee) the dominant position of men and the subordination of women".

Harding (1991) also notes that the creation of a "scientific method" that is apparently "value-free" and "objective", but which only considers objects of study from the standpoint of the dominant group, has meant that the voices of women, children, Black people, gay men, lesbians and disabled people have been obscured and ignored. The conventional approach in natural science, she states:

> ... fails to grasp that modern science has been constructed by and within power relations in society, not apart from them. The issue is not how one scientist or another used or abused social power in doing his (*sic*) science, but rather where the sciences and their agendas, concepts, and consequences have been located within particular currents of politics. How have their ideas and practices advanced some groups at the expense of others? (Harding, 1991, p. 81)

Similarly, Nicolson (1995, p. 123) has pointed out that: "Traditional academic experimental psychology employs reductionist methods, which set out to exclude both the social context and the structural/power relations between individuals as inherent 'bias'".

Thus, a critical perspective on the "scientific objectivity" embodied in mainstream social science reveals that it is merely the unacknowledged "standpoint" of White middle class heterosexual men and consequently that "scientific objectivity" merely (re)produces "knowledge" or a world-view that advances the interests of this particular group and ignores or dismisses the experiences of others (Harding, 1991; Lennon and Whitford, 1994; Nicolson, 1995). This perspective is particularly important when considering the nature of scientific discourse about sexual violence, for it may be that the interests of most men are served by the creation of a "classified" group of "sex offenders", the study of whom conveniently deflects attention from problematic aspects of hegemonic masculinity.

*Scientific Discourse – the Construction of the "Natural" Heterosexual Man*

In their overview of theoretical approaches to studying men, Edley and Wetherell (1995) identify the following approaches: biological, psychoanalytical, role theory, social relations, cultural and feminist. In considering the scientific discourse surrounding the construction of the "natural" man, the "biological" and "role theory" perspectives are particularly influential. Both are characterised by an "essentialist" approach to understanding human phenomena. Burr (1995, pp. 19-20) describes this approach as:

> ... a way of understanding the world that sees things (including human beings) as having their own particular essence or nature, something which is said to belong to them and which explains how they behave ... The "essentialist" view of personality, then, bids us think of ourselves as having a particular nature, both as individuals and as a species (i.e. "human nature"), and this nature determines what people can and cannot do.

The essentialism of biological and role theory approaches to studying male heterosexuality therefore holds that "man" is biologically predetermined to fulfil certain sexual roles, the secrets of which can be discovered by close, "objective", scientific study.

Foucault (1981) has drawn attention to the fact that, in Western societies, discussion about sexual behaviour has generally taken the form of "confession". Initially, this form of discourse was directed and controlled by the Church, but, from the mid-nineteenth century onwards, it has come to be dominated by "scientific" investigators, and particularly by the medical profession. In this section, I will consider the influence of the work of Havelock Ellis and later sexologists, including the work of the Kinsey Institute, in constructing "scientific" approaches to male heterosexuality, which at the same time assert the normality of male aggression and coercion in heterosexual activity and minimise the extent and effect of sexual violence.

Havelock Ellis was a late nineteenth/early twentieth century thinker and writer about sexual matters whose work is of key importance in the development of essentialist perspectives on male heterosexuality. Jeffrey

## "Normals" and "Offenders"

Weeks (2000, pp. 17-48) has usefully summarised Ellis's contribution to the study of human sexuality. In particular, Weeks highlights a tension in Ellis's work between a conservative and uncritical acceptance of the biological basis of sexual behaviour and a more radical use of evidence from a range of different times and cultures. It is his uncritical acceptance of predetermined heterosexual roles for men and women that is of particular concern in this paper. In *Studies in the Psychology of Sex*, published between 1900 and 1910, Ellis articulates his understanding of the basis of heterosexual behaviour:

> Force is the foundation of virility and its psychic manifestation is courage. In the struggles for life, violence is the first virtue. The modesty of women - in its primordial form consisting in physical resistance, active or passive, to the assaults of the male - aided selection by putting to the test man's most important quality, force. Thus it is that when choosing among rivals for her favours, a woman attributes value to violence (1903, p. 33; cited by Jackson, 1984, p. 57)

and

> The infliction of pain must inevitably be a frequent indirect result of the exertion of power (i.e. in courtship). It is even more than this; the infliction of pain by the male on the female may itself be a gratification of the impulse to exert force. (1903, p. 67; cited by Jackson, 1984, p. 58)

Ellis's essentialist understanding of heterosexual behaviours and the predetermined nature of male and female roles within this framework has been and remains influential.

Velde, for example, in his book *Ideal Marriage*, which was first published in English in 1928 and was reprinted over thirty-eight times in the next fifty years, states:

> What both man and woman, driven by obscure primitive urges, wish to feel in the act is the essential force of maleness, which expresses itself in a sort of violent and absolute possession of the woman. And so both of them can and do exult in a certain degree of male aggression and dominance, whether actual or apparent - which proclaims this actual force. (1977, p. 153; cited by Jackson, 1984, p. 65)

The work of Alfred Kinsey, and subsequently that of the Kinsey Institute, continued and developed the understanding of human sexuality embodied in the work of Havelock Ellis. Throughout their work, the facade of "objectivity" is both asserted and maintained. The works (Kinsey, Pomeroy, & Martin, 1948; Kinsey, Pomeroy, Martin & Gebhard, 1953; Gebhard, Gagnon, Pomeroy & Christenson, 1965) are "scientific" investigations into human sexual behaviours. All of the works, however, clearly reveal the value base and ideological orientation of the authors. Addressing the (male) context of sexual behaviours in which sexual "offences" have to be identified, Gebhard et al (1965, p. 177) note that:

## "Normals" and "Offenders"

... the phenomenon of force or threat in sexual relations between adults is beclouded by various things. In the first place, there may be the ambivalence of the female who is sexually aroused, but who for moral or other reasons does not wish to have coitus. She is struggling not only against the male, but against herself, and in retrospect it is exceedingly easy for her to convince herself that she yielded to force, rather than to persuasion. This delusion is facilitated by the socially approved pattern for feminine behaviour, according to which the woman is supposed to put up at least token resistance, murmuring "No, no" or "We mustn't". Any reasonably experienced male has learned to disregard such minor protestations, and the naive male who obeys his partner's injunction to cease and desist is often puzzled when she seems inexplicably irritated by his compliance.

Similar perspectives are to be found in two more recent reviews of understandings of rape. Ellis (1989) and Thornhill & Palmer (2000) assert essentialist understandings of male (and female) heterosexuality.

The distinction between "normal" male behaviour and that of the rapist becomes very difficult to distinguish. Emerging from essentialist perspectives of human sexuality is a view of male heterosexuality in which aggression and dominance are both "normal" and ineluctable. The distinction between "normal" male behaviour and "true" sex offences is, therefore, difficult to articulate. Thus, the extent of "offending behaviour" is difficult to estimate and male academics and clinicians erred on the side of extreme caution.

Salter (1988, p. 22) notes that, in the United States, "Clinicians trained as late as the 70s were instructed that sexual abuse was rare and cited figures for incest as low as one in a million ... ".

Similar viewpoints have been noted during the 1980s from some members of the British medical profession - for example, see Campbell (1988, pp. 55-60). It is, therefore, appropriate to consider the nature of these classification systems in some detail. The implication emerging strongly from this male dominated discourse is that there is only a small minority of men whose sexual behaviour is problematic.

*Forensic Science: Classification Systems*

It is within this context that sex offender classification systems began to emerge. The systems were developed in the male dominated "scientific" world of the "clinician" and were primarily considered an aid to diagnosis of men deemed to be "deviant".

There has been much effort expended on studying and classifying this small group of "deviant" men. Sex offenders are classified through two main types of typology – medical and psychological. I will consider these in turn and then, also, briefly consider the work of Diana Scully (1990), who developed a very different way of categorising rapists.

*Medical Approaches*

Medical classification of sex offending behaviour is guided and prescribed by two diagnostic manuals - the *International Classification of Diseases, Injuries and Causes of*

*Death (ICD)* of the World Health Organisation [WHO] (1992) and the *Diagnostic and Statistical Manual (DSM)* of the American Psychiatric Association [APA] (1995). The terminologies used to describe a variety of "deviant" sexual behaviours are complex and esoteric. There is little or no reference to a criminal justice context and there is a conspicuous absence of criminal justice terminology – the behaviours are categorised in medical language, without concern to the legal status of the behaviours. For example, in the current *ICD* -*ICD-10-* (1992), "deviant" sexual behaviours are described in a section entitled "Disorders of adult personality and behaviours". Some of the behaviours identified are fetishism, fetishistic transvestism, exhibitionism, voyeurism, paedophilia, sadomasochism, and multiple disorders of sexual preference.

The *Diagnostic and Statistical Manual (DSM-IV)* of the American Psychiatric Association (1995) is very similar in its orientation and focus. Interestingly, however, "Deviant sexual behaviours" are included in the section on "Gender identity disorders" in a sub-section entitled "Paraphilias". Men and masculinity/(ies) are, however, not referred to.

The "deviant" behaviours are labelled with technical descriptors and, although the use of force and the effect on others is noted ("humiliation or suffering"), it is solely as a phenomenological aspect of the "paraphilia". There are no explicit links to legal definitions and no consideration of the dynamics of power in relationships.

*Psychological Approaches*

These systems are based on knowledge about convicted men. All of the systems isolate offenders who have abused children (the more common North American word is "molested") from offenders who have raped adults (women). I will briefly review the main characteristics of these systems. However, for a more comprehensive review of these taxonomies, see Fisher and Mair (1998).

*Child Molesters*

A common feature of these classification systems is a tripartite division of the different types of offender, commonly referred to as "paedophiles" (Knight, Rosenberg, and Schneider, 1985; Knight 1988; Knight, Carter, and Prentky, 1989). The systems highlight the following categories:

- "Fixated paedophiles", who have a specific and often longstanding sexual preference for children (Cohen, Boucher, Seghorn, and Mehegan, 1979; Groth, Longo, and McFadin, 1982);
- "Regressed paedophiles", who engage in sexual activity with children, particularly in family settings, as a result of external pressures; and
- "Unskilled psychopaths", who may have an identifiable psychiatric disorder, who are generally unskilled socially and who choose children because they are easier to exploit.

Although the above forms the basic infrastructure for classification systems of "child molesters", more elaborate systems have been developed that take into account both offence demographics (i.e. the nature of the offence and the age and sex of the victim) and the meaning of the behaviour of the offender (Knight, 1988; Knight, Carter, and Prentky,1989; Knight and Prentky, 1990).

*Rapists*

Classification systems of rapists originate in the 1950s. Most of the systems identify similar "types". They primarily consider the underlying motivation for rape and the personality characteristics of the rapists.

Groth, Burgess, and Holmstrom (1977) identified two main categories of rape – "power rape" and "anger rape". They then further divided each category – power rapists could be either "power-reassurance" rapists or rapists who rape to express their potency. On the other hand, anger rapists use rape to humiliate and degrade their victims and this category is further sub-divided into "anger-retaliation" and "anger-excitement". In later work, Groth appears to have refined his typologies and suggests three main groups – "anger", "power" and "sadistic" rape (Groth and Birnbaum, 1979).

Cohen, Garofolo, Boucher, and Seghorn (1971) suggest the following taxonomy - compensatory, impulsive, displaced aggressive and sex-aggression defusion - and consider that it was likely that individuals would be distributed along the discriminating dimensions rather than fall into discrete categories.

Knight and Prentky (1990) describe the development of the Massachusetts Treatment Center (Rapists 3) Typology [MTC:R3] from studying the rapists in the Treatment Center. This typology has four main motivational categories: opportunistic; pervasively angry; sexual; and vindictive; but, taking account of explicitly stated levels and degrees of expressive aggression, juvenile and adult unsocialised behaviour, social competence, sexualisation, undifferentiated anger, sadism and offence planning, it identifies nine sub-groupings.

Fisher and Mair (1998, p. 27) note:

> The fact that there is such consistency of types identified by different studies suggests that these types are both valid and stable. ... Specific data on the reliability, homogeneity and coverage of these systems is not reported ... In addition, it is of note that at the

time of these studies the phenomenon of rape in marriage and date rape was not particularly recognised. Whilst it is likely that such acts would be classed as being sexually motivated, they do not easily fit the subgroups identified ... and as such represent an important omission.

And, possibly, many other "unreported" sex crimes similarly fail to fit into the classification systems.

*Sociological Perspectives*

Diana Scully, a feminist sociologist, studied men convicted of rape who were imprisoned in a maximum-security prison in the United States (Scully, 1990). Rather than use the psychological classification systems, she developed a different system, " ... based on their versions of their crimes, and the information contained in their records" (p. 27). The categories that she identified are: "admitters"; "deniers"; and those who claimed no knowledge of the offence(s). She omitted the third grouping from her discussion. "Admitters" admitted that they had committed the offence(s) with which they were charged, although their accounts of their offences minimised their use of violence. The second group, the "deniers", admitted that they had been sexually involved with their victim(s), but denied the coercive nature of the activity. Scully notes that there are a number of ways in which their denial could be interpreted, but adds: "... denials can also be taken at face value, and the content analyzed as a statement on the cultural learning and socially derived perspective of sexually violent men" (p. 28).

## "Normals" and "Offenders"

Summarising the issues emerging from analysing the deniers accounts, Scully (1990, p. 115) comments:

> To justify their behavior, deniers drew on the stereotypes of women in our rape-supportive culture to present their victims as both precipitating and to blame for the rapes. ... Six themes run through denier's accounts, each constructed so that the victim and her behavior is presented in such a way that the man's behavior seemed situationally appropriate or justified – even if not quite right: (1) women as seductresses; (2) women mean "yes" when they say "no"; (3) women eventually "relax and enjoy it"; (4) nice girls don't get raped; (5) guilty of minor wrong doing; and (6) macho man.

It is worthy of note that, with the exception of Scully's study, none of the systems reviewed pays particular attention to the gender of the offenders and how this relates to the patriarchal structure of the societies in which the offences were committed. Generally, they focus on a relatively small group of convicted men. This can have the unfortunate effect of creating the illusion that sexual violence is a relatively insignificant feature of social life and it is the activity of a prolific, but small, group of men. Consideration of statistics related to sexual offending and the experience of being victimised seriously undermines this false security.

*Statistics Relating to Sex Offending: the Number and Patterns of Convictions*

Given that classification systems are generally derived from what is known about the behaviour of convicted sex offenders, it is important to review some of this literature. This is not to revert to a natural science perspective on quantitative data – i.e. it represents the "truth". Plummer (1995, p. 19), in citing the work of Clough (1992), has noted that: " ... all factual representation of empirical reality, even statistics, are narratively constructed".

Generally, official crime statistics relating to sexual violence tell an understated story of (a) increasing numbers of sex crimes reported, and (b) some (few) persistent offenders. In citing this body of work, I am seeking to disturb the conventional narrative and highlight an alternative tale, which problematizes, more generally, male heterosexuality. It is also important to recognise that, by referring to official statistics, the information provided is constrained by official definitions of sex crimes. To some extent, I compensate for this later in the chapter when I consider the literature relating to prevalence studies, where different definitions of sex crimes are used.

Features that are of particular importance to the alternative tale that I seek to develop are: (i) the continual increase in the number of reported sex offences; (ii) rates of recidivism for sex offenders; (iii) rates of recidivism for sex offenders with no previous convictions; and (iv) the proportion of sex offenders without convictions cited in the literature.

## "Normals" and "Offenders"

*(i) The Continual Increase in the Number of Reported Sex Offences*

Official statistics over the last twenty years have revealed a slow, but marked, increase in the number of convictions for sexual offences. In Britain, the number of sexual offences has increased from 17,954 in 1981 to 28,245 in 1991 (Marshall, 1994). Colton and Vanstone (1998) also demonstrate a similar increase in numbers of reported sex offences.

*(ii) Rates of Recidivism for Sex Offenders*

The popular view that sex offenders invariably re-offend is, however, contradicted by research findings. In a review of sixty-one studies undertaken in Europe and North America from 1943 to 1995, Hanson and Bussiere (1998, p. 357) noted that, as a group, sex offenders have a low rate of recidivism:

> Only a minority of the total sample (13.4% of 23, 393) were known to have committed a new sexual offence within the average 4-5 year follow-up ... even in studies with thorough record searches and long follow-up periods (15-20 years), the recidivism rates almost never exceed 40%.

Recidivism rates also vary when the type of offence is considered: incest offenders, 4-10%; rapists, 7-35%; non-familial child abusers, 10-29% against females and 13-40% against boys (Marshall and Barbaree, 1990; cited in Fisher, 1994, p. 12). Additionally, the number of previous convictions appears to affect the rate at which offenders are subsequently reconvicted. Hanson and Bussiere (1998) point out that offenders may be re-offending and not being caught, but this is an unknown. However, Soothill, Francis, and Ackerley (1998) have suggested that, given the length of time of follow-up in many recidivism studies (10-20 years), it is unlikely that the re-offences of a known sex offender would remain concealed for this length of time.

### iii) Rates of Recidivism for Sex Offenders with No Previous Convictions

The figure that is of particular interest in the present context relates to men convicted of sex offences for the first time. Gibbens, Soothill, and Way (1978) found that 12% of the first offenders were reconvicted within ten years. Similarly, Phillpotts and Lancucki (1979) noted that, within a six-year follow-up period, only 1.5% of sex offenders with no previous convictions were convicted of a further sexual offence. West (1987, p. 18) notes that: "It is a common misapprehension that sex offenders are very liable to repeated convictions. Certainly some of them are, but that is not the general rule. The typical sex offender appears in court once only and never again".

Many other commentators (Furby, Weinrott, and Blackshaw, 1989; Quinsey, 1984, 1986; Howard League for Penal Reform, 1985) have also drawn attention to this feature of sex offender recidivism. The Howard League Working Party (1985, p. 17) similarly notes:

> Although sex offenders are often credited with being particularly persistent in their misbehaviour, in fact, it is only a small minority who reappear repeatedly in court on sex charges; the vast majority

have only one conviction for a sex offence in the whole of their lives.

*iv) The Proportion of Sex Offenders Without Convictions Cited in the Literature*

Apart from the relatively low recidivism rates of convicted sex offenders, a rarely commented upon feature in these studies is that the majority of sex offenders in each sample *do not* have previous convictions for sexual offences. This finding has been consistently affirmed in a number of studies over a period of time. For example, Radzinowicz's (1957) study revealed that 83% had no previous convictions for sexual offences. Fitch (1962) found that 79% of the 77 heterosexual offenders had no previous convictions for sexual offending; but 52% of the 62 homosexual offenders had had prior sexual convictions. Gibbens, Soothill, and Way's (1978) work showed that 87% of their sample had no previous convictions for sexual offences. In 1981, Gibbens, Soothill, and Way noted that 89% of the sample had no previous convictions for sexual offences. Cowburn's (1991) research on 233 male sex offenders in prison confirmed that 64% had no previous conviction for sexual offences; and Marshall's (1994) study of sex offenders discharged from the prisons of England and Wales indicated that 73% had no previous convictions.

To summarise, this data offers a picture of low re-conviction rates for convicted sex offenders and very low numbers of offenders with previous convictions. In the studies cited above, the vast majority of offenders have no previous convictions and are not subsequently re-convicted, yet the number of reported sex crimes is increasing. This may be due to an increase in the numbers of people reporting crimes or an increase in sexually coercive behaviour. Official statistics relating to sexual crimes, based on the number of convictions for sex offences, significantly under-represent both the incidence and the prevalence of acts of sexual abuse (see, for example, Quinsey, 1984; Finkelhor, 1986; Quinsey, 1986; Kelly, 1988; Kelly, Regan & Burton, 1991; Glaser & Frosh, 1993; Fisher, 1994). As mentioned above, the very definitions used by "official" sources may inhibit or prevent behaviours being reported (see the reference to Kelly, Regan & Burton, 1991, below). I will now consider other studies that have examined other sources of information.

*Prevalence Studies*

It is now almost a truism to state that the number of convictions for sexual offences represents the "tip of the iceberg" of sexual offending behaviour. Various surveys conducted with sample populations, both in Britain and in the United States, have revealed that the prevalence of people who have been sexually attacked at some point in their lives is significantly higher than the recorded number of convictions for sexual offences. Donald West (1987, p. 12) notes:

> According to the results of the Home Office National Crime Survey, in which members of a representative sample of households were asked about their experiences of victimisation, only about one in ten rapes or sexual assaults on women had been reported to police.

In the Report of the Howard League Working Party (1985, p. 12), the authors quote earlier research:

## "Normals" and "Offenders"

> Figures from the recent British Crime Survey (1983) ... suggest that only one quarter of the offences of indecent assault upon women of sixteen years or older which took place in 1981 were officially recorded. Data from the National Opinion Research Centre in Canada also suggested that reported rapes amounted to only a quarter of the figure obtained from self-reports ...

Salter (1988) reviews both "recent" (1979-1989) and "older" (1929-1965) prevalence studies with regard to child sexual abuse. She excludes from the review studies of sexual abuse in clinical settings, because they (inevitably) reveal artificially high prevalence rates. She found that the recent studies revealed that between 11% and 39% of the women had been abused, whilst the range for men was between 5% and 11%. The "older" prevalence studies, Salter (1988, p. 21) acknowledges, " ... lack the sophisticated methodology and the careful definitions of more recent research." However, they reveal rates of sexual abuse of female children ranging from 24% to 37% and, although only two of the studies consider the disclosure rate of abuse for males, these rates are 27% and 30%. Salter states that sexual abuse, and particularly child sexual abuse, is *not* a recent discovery.

Other studies of the prevalence of sexual violence in sample populations reveal a wide range of prevalence rates; (see the following literature reviews: Quinsey, 1984; Quinsey, 1986; Finkelhor, 1986; Salter, 1988; Birchall, 1989; Stermac, Segal and Gillis, 1990; and Conte, 1991). These vary for females from 8% to 41%. In their study of the prevalence of sexual abuse in a sample of British 16-21 year olds, Kelly, Regan and Burton (1991) found that one in two females and one in four males had experienced at least one unwanted sexual event/interaction before they were eighteen. Having taken "less serious" incidents out of their analysis, they found that one in five women and one in fourteen males reported having experienced "serious" abuse. The prevalence rates were the same for both Black and White young people. Only 5% of the incidents were reported to any agency and of these (1,051), only 10 resulted in prosecution.

On the basis of their extensive review of the literature, Percy and Mayhew (1997) estimate that there are 15 times more unreported sex offenders than reported ones; the bulk of sex offenders have not been brought to public notice; and their offences remain unacknowledged in the private domain.

This prompts consideration of other studies that relate to "the private domain". The area that is most fertile is studies where men have been asked, in conditions of total confidentiality, about their attitudes relating to sexual violence and their proclivities to committing such acts.

*Proclivities to Sexual Violence: Men Self-Reporting*

The difference between "normals" and sex offenders becomes less clear when we consider research that examines the attitudes about and proclivities towards sexual violence in populations of "normal" adult men. Most of these studies use samples of White middle-class college students in the United States. Although they cannot be regarded as representative of the general population, this research reveals that a significant proportion of "normal" men have pro-rape attitudes and proclivities.

Malamuth (1981) estimated that 35% of college males reported the likelihood of rape, even if not assured of not being caught or punished. The male subjects in Petty and

## "Normals" and "Offenders"

Dawson's 1989 study reported that they considered it unlikely that they would be caught and punished if they did carry out a rape. Rapaport and Burkhart (1984) found that 28% of college males had engaged in coercive sexual activity. Muehlenhard and Linton (1987) reported that over 77% of college females had been involved as victims and 50% of college males as perpetrators of sexually abusive acts. Kanin (1969) found that approximately 25% of university males admitted using force in attempted intercourse, even when they knew it was not wanted and distressing. Kanin (1985) revealed that 13% of males from a variety of university classes reported using force or threats to obtain coitus from a female. Stermac, Segal, and Gillis (1990, p. 146), reviewing this literature, noted: "A fairly consistent finding of approximately 30-35% of the males across the studies indicated that there was some likelihood they would rape under these conditions".

Regarding attitudes towards acceptability of rape, Goodchilds and Zellman (1984) found that the majority of males in their high school sample reported that "date rape" was acceptable under a variety of circumstances.

A significant number of studies also reveal that similar attitudes prevail with regard to male arousal over, or abuse of, children. For example, Briere and Runtz (1989) found that 21% of college males reported having some sexual attraction to children and 7% reported some likelihood of having sex with a child if they could ensure not being detected or punished. Finkelhor and Lewis (1988) estimated that 10% of males from a sample of their telephone survey had admitted having sexually abused a child.

These studies, cumulatively, raise serious concerns about hegemonic masculinity: (note that most of them were undertaken in White-dominated, middle class universities). Yet, cloaked in the language of "scientific" discourse, they have remained largely uncommented on, outside of the "scientific" community. Other voices have, albeit briefly, reached a wider audience.

*Feminist Critiques of Male Heterosexuality*

Both the so-called first and second "waves" of feminism in the twentieth century highlighted problems with male heterosexual behaviour. Whilst Ellis was writing of the "natural" predatory nature of male heterosexuality, Jackson (1984, p. 50) states that:

> Women such as Josephine Butler, Elizabeth Wollstenholme, Jane Ellice Hopkins, Frances Swiney, and later Cicely Hamilton and Christabel Pankhurst, challenged the myth that the sexual abuse and exploitation of women and girls was an unfortunate but inevitable result of men's natural sexual urges. They clearly saw male sexuality as a consequence of male power, not male biology, and they demanded that men exercise self-control.

Similarly, writers in the second "wave" were also critical of perspectives that minimised the extent and the effect of sexual violence and cast serious doubt on the validity of the distinction between "normal" men and "deviant" men (Brownmiller, 1975; Davis, 1981; Hanmer and Saunders, 1984; Dworkin, 1981; Dworkin, 1987; Dominelli, 1991; Hanmer, 1990).

*A Way Forward*

> Thus, modern Western science was construed within and by political agendas that contained both liberatory and oppressive

## "Normals" and "Offenders"

possibilities. Present-day science too contains these conflicting impulses. The anti-democratic impulses are not only morally and politically problematic; *they also deteriorate the ability of the sciences to provide objective, empirically defensible descriptions and explanations of the regularities and underlying causal tendencies in nature and social relations* [italics added]. One way to focus on this problem is to discover that we have no conception of objectivity that enables us to distinguish the scientifically "best descriptions and explanations" from those that fit most closely (intentionally or not) with the assumptions that elites in the West do not want critically examined.

(Harding, 1991, p. 97)

This paper has shown how the "scientific" study of male heterosexuality and male sex offenders potentially produces descriptions and explanations that fit most closely with the assumptions of the dominant grouping in Western society – White, middle class, able-bodied, heterosexual men. This particular approach creates a situation that minimises the nature and extent of sexual violence by:

(a) Constructing male heterosexuality as potentially aggressive and coercive, but also "natural" and therefore uncontroversial; and

(b) Developing an understanding of sexual violence by studying only men who have been convicted of sexual offences. This perpetuates the myth that perpetrators of "true" sexual offences are a minority "deviant" group who need to be identified (as separate from ordinary men) and "scientifically" classified and "treated". It is this group that preoccupies the interest and attention of the (mostly male) makers of social policy.

At the same time, however, the following features that problematize dominant approaches to sexual violence are largely ignored (particularly by policy makers):

(a) Reported incidents of sexual violence are increasing and therefore, following Percy and Mayhew (1997), unreported incidents also may be increasing;

(b) The little noted phenomenon that the majority of sex offenders are only convicted once;

(c) Male self-report studies of proclivities to behave in sexually coercive ways indicate that a substantial minority of men are willing to do so.

(d) Feminist critiques of male power.

It appears that, if social policy is to be concerned with creating a safer society for everyone, it will need to find a way of incorporating a wider range of perspectives about the nature of both sexual violence and also dominant forms of masculinity. Essentialist understandings of these phenomena, which are formed from an uncritical and unacknowledged male dominated science, are clearly inadequate. To devote resources – in terms of research, treatment programmes and incarceration – solely to this narrowly defined group may well be seriously to miss the point.

In writing of convicted rapists and the ways in which they minimise their behaviour, Scully (1990, p. 116) highlights the difficulties for patriarchal societies in combating sexual violence: " ... patriarchal societies produce men whose frame of reference excludes women's perspectives; men are able to ignore sexual violence, especially since their culture provides them with such a convenient array of justifications".

This points to a reconsideration of the notion of male hegemony in Western societies. Moving away from fixed essentialist understandings of masculinity and moving towards social relations and cultural perspectives, masculinity is construed as something that is negotiated and "performed" (see also Butler [1989] for arguments that gender is fundamentally a performative act). As such, it is open to challenge and change; but, before change is possible, focuses for change need to be identified. Mac an Ghaill (1994, p. 96), in his study of "Parnell" comprehensive school in the Midlands of England, noted that: " ... male students at Parnell School learn to be men in terms of three constitutive elements of compulsory heterosexuality, misogyny and homophobia".

This can be regarded as a toxic and contradictory combination. Scully (1990, p. 9) also indicated the relationship between the behaviours of male prisoners in her study and hegemonic/traditional expectations of men:

> Externally, at least, traditional male role behavior is exaggerated [in prison]. Manhood is validated through physical strength and aggression. Expressions like anger are expected and acceptable, but emotional sensitivity to others or the appearance of caring is regarded as dangerous. Any display of characteristics or behavior traditionally associated with the feminine is scorned and avoided.

Jackson (1990, p. 124) has also identified that: "'Hard case' masculinity not only defines itself positively through assertiveness, virility, toughness, independence, etc., but also negatively by defining itself in opposition to what it is not - feminine or homosexual".

Some convicted and ordinary men, it would appear,

share some key attitudes. The simple equation: misogyny, plus compulsory heterosexuality, plus homophobia, would appear to have only one logical product – heterosexual violence. However, I am not suggesting that the "constituent" parts of masculinities identified above are fixed and immutable; to do so would be to regress to an essentialist position. However, independent commentators have identified these aspects to the social performance of masculinities in a variety of settings, with a variety of groups of men. Thus, a way forward in effectively reducing the presence of sexual violence may lie, not in developing increasingly sophisticated forensic understandings of the convicted population, but in developing research programmes and social policy initiatives that examine and challenge hegemonic values and behaviours that nurture and sustain harmful masculinities.

*References*

American Psychiatric Association (1995). *Diagnostic and statistical manual of mental disorders: [DSM-I]*. Washington, DC: Author.

Birchall, E. (1989). The frequency of child abuse: What do we really know? In O. Stevenson (Ed.), *Child abuse: Professional practice and public policy* (pp. 1-27). London: Harvester Wheatsheaf.

Briere, J., & Runtz, M. (1989). University males' sexual interest in children: Predicting potential indices of "paedophilia" in a nonforensic sample. *Child Abuse and Neglect, 13,* 65-75.

Brownmiller, S. (1975). *Against our will: Men, women and rape.* London: Secker and Warburg.

Burr, V. (1995). *An introduction to social constructionism.* London: Routledge.

Butler, J. (1989). *Gender trouble: Feminism and the subversion of identity.* New York: Routledge.

Campbell, B. (1988). *Unofficial secrets: Child sex abuse: The Cleveland case.* London: Virago.

Clough, P. T. (1992). *The end (s) of ethnography: from realism to social criticism.* Newbury Park, CA: Sage.

Cohen, M. L., Boucher, R. J., Seghorn, T., & Mehegan, J. (1979). *The sexual offender against children.* Boston, MA: The Association for Professional Treatment of Offenders.

Cohen, M. L., Garofolo, R., Boucher, R. J., & Seghorn, T. (1971). The psychology of rapists. *Seminars in psychiatry, 3,* 307-327.

Colton, M., & Vanstone, M. (1998). Sexual abuse by men who work with children: An exploratory study. *British Journal of Social Work, 28,* 511-523.

Connell, R. W. (1995). *Masculinities.* Cambridge: Polity Press.

Conte, J. R. (1991). The nature of sexual offences against children. In C. R. Hollin & K. Howells (Eds.), *Clinical approaches to sex offenders and their victims* (pp. 11-34). Chichester, John Wiley.

Cowburn, M. (1991). *Sex offenders in prison: A study of structured interventions to change offending behaviour.* Unpublished M. Phil. thesis, University of Nottingham.

Davis, A. (1981). *Women, race & class.* London: Women's Press.

Dominelli, L. (1991). *Gender, sex offenders and probation practice.* Norwich, Novata Press.

Dworkin, A. (1981). *Pornography: Men possessing women.* London, Women's Press.

Dworkin, A. (1987). *Intercourse.* London, Secker & Warburg.

Edley, N., & Wetherell, M. (1995). *Men in perspective: Practice, power and identity.* London: Prentice Hall/Harvester Wheatsheaf.

Ellis, H. (1900). *Studies in the psychology of sex. Volume 1.* Philadelphia: F. A. Davis Co.

Ellis, H. (1901). *Studies in the psychology of sex. Volume 2.* Philadelphia: F. A. Davis Co.

Ellis, H. (1903). *Studies in the psychology of sex. Volume 3.* Philadelphia: F. A. Davis Co.

Ellis, H. (1905). *Studies in the psychology of sex. Volume 4.* Philadelphia: F. A. Davis Co.

Ellis, H. (1906). *Studies in the psychology of sex. Volume 5.* Philadelphia: F. A. Davis Co.

Ellis, H. (1910). *Studies in the psychology of sex. Volume 6.* Philadelphia: F. A. Davis Co.

Ellis, L. (1989). *Theories of rape: Inquiries into the causes of sexual aggression.* New York: Hemisphere.

Finkelhor, D., Araji, S., Baron, L., Browne, A., Peters, S. D., & Wyatt, G. E. (1986). *A sourcebook on child sexual abuse.* Newbury Park, CA: Sage.

Finkelhor, D., & Lewis, I. S. (1988). An epidemiologic approach to the study of child molestation. In R. A. Prentky & V. L. Quinsey (Eds.), *Human sexual aggression: Current perspectives.* New York: New York Academy of Sciences.

Fisher, D. (1994). Adult sex offenders: Who are they? Why and how do they do it? In T. Morrison, M. Erooga & R. C. Beckett (Eds.), *Sexual offending against children:*

*Assessment and treatment of male abusers* (pp. 1-24). London: Routledge.

Fisher, D., & Mair, G. (1998). *A review of classification schemes for sex offenders.* Edinburgh: Scottish Office, Central Research Unit.

Fitch, J. (1962). Men convicted of sexual offences against children: A descriptive follow-up study. *British Journal of Criminology, 3,* 18-37.

Foucault, M. (1981). *The history of sexuality: An introduction* (R. Hurley, Trans.). Harmondsworth: Penguin. (Original work published 1976)

Furby, L., Weinrott, M. R., & Blackshaw, L. (1989). Sex offender recidivism: A review. *Psychological Bulletin, 105* (1), 3-30.

Gebhard, P. H., Gagnon, J. H., Pomeroy, W. B. & Christenson, C. V. (1965). *Sex offenders: An analysis of types.* New York: Harper and Row.

Gibbens, T. C. N., Soothill, K. L., & Way, C. K. (1978). Sibling and parent-child incest offenders. *British Journal of Criminology, 18,* 40-52.

Gibbens, T. C. N., Soothill, K. L., & Way, C. K. (1981). Sex offences against young girls: A long-term record study. *Psychological Medicine, 11,* 351-357.

Glaser, D., & Frosh, S. (1993). *Child sexual abuse.* (2nd ed.) Basingstoke: Macmillan.

Goodchilds, J., & Zellman, G. (1984). Sexual signalling and sexual aggression in adolescent relationships. In N. M. Malamuth & E. Donnerstein (Eds.). *Pornography and sexual aggression.* Orlando, FL: Academic Press.

Groth, A. N., & Birnbaum, H. J. (1979). *Men who rape: The psychology of the offender.* New York: Plenum Press.

Groth, A. N., Burgess, A. W., & Holmstrom, L. L. (1977). Rape: Power, anger and sexuality. *American Journal of Psychiatry, 134,* 1239-1243.

Groth, A. N., Longo, R. E., & McFadin. J. B. (1982). Undetected recidivism in rapists and child molesters. *Crime and Delinquency, 28,* 450-458.

Hanmer, J. (1990). Men, power and the exploitation of women. In J. Hearn & D. H. J. Morgan (Eds.), *Men, masculinities and social theory.* London: Unwin Hyman.

Hanmer, J., & Saunders, S. (1984). *Well-founded fear: A community study of violence to women.* London: Hutchinson.

Hanson, R., & Bussiere, M. T. (1998). Predicting relapse: A meta-analysis of sexual offender recidivism studies.

*Journal of Counselling and Clinical Psychology,* 66 (2), 348-362.

Harding, S. (1991). *Whose science? Whose knowledge? Thinking from women's lives.* Buckingham: Open University Press.

Hearn, J. (1998). Theorizing men and men's theorizing: Varieties of discursive practices in men's theorizing of men. *Theory and Society,* 27, 781-816.

Howard League for Penal Reform (1985). *Unlawful sex: Offences, victims and offenders in the criminal justice system of England and Wales: The report of a Howard League working party.* London: Waterlow.

Jackson, D. (1990). *Unmasking masculinity: A critical autobiography.* London: Unwin Hyman.

Jackson, M. (1984). Sexology and the social construction of male sexuality (Havelock Ellis). In L. Coveney, M. Jackson, S. Jeffreys, L. Kaye & P. Mahony (Eds.) *The Sexuality Papers: Male sexuality and the social control of women.* London: Hutchinson.

Kanin, E. J. (1969). Selected dyadic aspects of male sex aggression. *Journal of Sex Research,* 5, 12-28.

Kanin, E. J. (1985). Date rapists: differential sexual socialization and relative deprivation. *Archives of Sexual Behavior, 6,* 67 -76.

Kelly, L. (1988). *Surviving sexual violence.* Cambridge: Polity Press.

Kelly, L., Regan, L., & Burton, S. (1991). *An exploratory study of the prevalence of sexual abuse in a sample of 16-21 year olds.* London: Polytechnic of North London, Child Abuse Studies Unit.

Kinsey, A. C., Pomeroy, W. B., & Martin, C. E. (1948). *Sexual behavior in the human male.* Philadelphia: W. B. Saunders Co.

Kinsey, A. C., Pomeroy, W. B., Martin, C. E., & Gebhard, P. H. (1953). *Sexual behavior in the human female.* Philadelphia: W. B. Saunders Co.

Knight, R. (1988). A taxonomic analysis of child molesters. In R. A. Prentky & V. L. Quinsey (Eds.), *Human sexual aggression: current perspectives.* New York, Annals of the New York Academy of Sciences, 528, 2-20.

Knight, R., Carter, D., & Prentky, R. (1989). A system for the classification of child molesters. *Journal of Interpersonal Violence, 4,* 3-23.

Knight, R., & Prentky, R. (1990). The development and corroboration of taxonomic models. In W. L. Marshall, D. R. Laws & H. E. Barbaree (Eds.), *Handbook of sexual assault: Issues, theories, and treatment of the offender.* New York: Plenum Press.

Knight, R., Rosenberg, R., & Schneider, B. A. (1985). Classification of sexual offenders: Perspectives, methods, and validation. In A. W. Burgess (Ed.), *Rape and sexual assault: A research handbook, [1].* New York: Garland.

Laws, D. R. (1994). How dangerous are rapists to children? *The Journal of Sexual Aggression, 1* (1), 1-14.

Lennon, K., & Whitford, M. (Eds.) (1994). *Knowing the difference: Feminist perspectives in epistemology.* London: Routledge.

Mac an Ghaill, M. (1994). *The making of men: Masculinities, sexualities, and schooling.* Buckingham: Open University Press.

Malamuth, N. (1981). Rape proclivity among males. *Journal of Social Issues, 37,* 138-157.

Marshall, P. (1994). *Reconviction of imprisoned sexual offenders.* London: Home Office.

Marshall, W. L., & Barbaree, H.E. (1990). Outcome of comprehensive treatment programs. In W. L. Marshall, D. R. Laws & H. E. Barbaree (Eds.), *Handbook of sexual assault: Issues, theories and treatment of the offender* (pp. 363-388). New York: Plenum Press.

Muehlenhard, C. L., & Linton, M. A. (1987). Date rape and sexual aggression in dating situations: Incidence and risk factors. *Journal of Counselling Psychology, 34*, 186-196.

Nicolson, P. (1995). Feminism and psychology. In J. A. Smith, R. Harre & L. Van Langenhove (Eds.), *Rethinking psychology* (pp. 122-142). London: Sage.

Percy, A., & Mayhew, P. (1997). Estimating sexual victimisation in a national crime survey: A new approach. *Studies on crime and crime prevention, 6* (2), 355-362.

Petty, G., & Dawson, B. (1989). Sexual aggression in normal men: Incidence, beliefs and personality characteristics. *Personality and Individual Differences, 10,* (3), 355-362.

Phillpotts, G. J. O., & Lancucki, L. B. (1979). *Previous convictions, sentence, and reconvictions: A statistical study of a sample of 5000 offenders convicted in January 1971.* London: HMSO.

Plummer, K. (1995). *Telling sexual stories: Power, change and social worlds.* London: Routledge.

Quinsey, V. L. (1984). Sexual aggression: Studies of offenders against women. In D. N. Weisstub (Ed.), *Law and mental health: International perspectives, 1.* New York: Pergamon Press.

Quinsey, V. L. (1986). Men who have sex with children. In D. N. Weisstub (Ed.), *Law and mental health: International perspectives, 2.* New York: Pergamon Press.

Radzinowicz, L. (Ed.) (1957). *Sexual offences: A report of the Cambridge Department of Criminal Science.* London: Macmillan.

Rapaport, K., & Burkhart, B. (1984). Personality and attitudinal characteristics of sexually coercive college males. *Journal of Abnormal Psychology, 93,* 216-221.

Salter, A. C. (1988). *Treating child sex offenders and victims: A practical guide.* Beverly Hills, CA: Sage.

Scully, D. (1990). *Understanding sexual violence: A study of convicted rapists.* Boston, MA: Unwin Hyman.

Soothill, K. L., Francis, B., & Ackerley, E. (1998, June 12). Paedophilia and paedophiles. *New Law Journal,* 882-883.

Stermac, L. E., Segal, Z. V., & Gillis, R. (1990). Social and cultural factors in sexual assault. In W. L. Marshall, D.

R. Laws & H. E. Barbaree (Eds.), *Handbook of sexual assault: Issues, theories and treatment of the offender*. New York: Plenum Press.

Thornhill, R., & Palmer, C. T. (2000). *A natural history of rape: Biological bases of sexual coercion*. Cambridge, MA: MIT Press.

Velde, T. H. van de (1977). *Ideal marriage: Its physiology and technique*. London: Mayflower. (Original English translation published 1928).

Weeks, J. (2000). *Making sexual history*. Cambridge: Polity Press.

West, D. J. (1987). *Sexual crimes and confrontations: A study of victims and offenders*. Aldershot, Gower.

World Health Organisation (1992). *The ICD-10 classification of mental and behavioural disorders : clinical descriptions and diagnostic guidelines*. Geneva: Author.

3

# "MY WIFE'S TONGUE DELIVERS MORE PUNISHING BLOWS THAN MUHAMMED ALI'S FIST"[1]: BARGAINING POWER IN NIGERIAN HAUSA SOCIETY

Fatima L. Adamu

*Introduction*

The concept and issue of power is very relevant in understanding and challenging the different dimensions of domination that women experience in the family, workplace, economy, politics, and in the activities of our everyday lives. Equal in importance is our interest in understanding the power that women have and exercise in response to such domination. The focus of this paper is on the latter. That is, it is an exploration of the power that women have and exercise in their relationships with men in a Muslim society in Northern Nigeria. Moore (1994) and Kandiyoti (1998) note that women use a variety of strategies in their daily interactions with men to contest and resist male power and domination. As the title of this paper suggests, the focus here is on the use of the social dimension of power by women to challenge their subordination and to bargain with men. Consequently, power is viewed in this paper both as a resource that an individual can possess and, in relational terms, that she/he can exercise over another person.

---

[1] Salamone, F. A., (1976), "The arrow and the bird: Proverbs in the solution of Hausa conjugal conflict", *Journal of Anthropological Research*, volume 32, pp. 358-371

"My Wife's Tongue ... "

The paper is divided into four sections. The first section provides the theoretical framework on which it is based and this is followed in section two by background information on Hausa society, providing the social context. The third part of the paper provides an analysis of the dynamics and complexity of power relationships between men and women - that is, the power women draw upon to challenge and bargain with men and the nature of such bargaining - and the final part provides a conclusion.

The data in this paper is largely drawn from six month's fieldwork conducted in Sokoto State, Northern Nigeria, in 1998. The concern of the research was an exploration and analysis of household dynamics in a period of economic crisis. The research methods used were largely qualitative.

*Theoretical Framework*

In view of the complexity surrounding power both as a theoretical and an analytical construct, we shall briefly provide the framework upon which power is used and viewed in this paper. To provide this framework, we have adopted Amy Allen's (1999) three perspectives on power. She provides us with an excellent analysis of power, as viewed from the existing feminist theory and gender studies literature. The first perspective views power as a social resource that can be possessed, distributed and redistributed. Accordingly, this perspective views the current distribution of power between men and women in most societies as unequal and therefore in need of redistribution. The subordinate social position of women is therefore attributed to their lack of equal access to power and other resources in the society. The task ahead of women activists and feminists is to struggle for the redistribution of power, both in the private sphere of the family and in the public arena of politics, religion and economy, so that women's access to power and resources will become equal to that of men.

The second perspective sees power as a relationship of male domination and female subordination, through which gender relations are created and reinforced. The task here, for women activists, is not to enable women to have power equal that of men, but to dismantle the whole system and structure of domination. The third perspective views power as empowerment, the capacity women have to transform and empower themselves, others and the world, rather than to control others. This perspective emerges as a critique of the previous two views, particularly their failure to account for the power that women have and exercise, despite their subordination, and their ability to resist male domination. This perspective considers the domination, resistance and empowerment of women as complexly inter-related. In short: where there is power, there is counter-power; and where there is domination, there will be resistance.

In this paper, therefore, power is viewed in this multi-dimensional way. It is this complex interrelationship of domination and resistance that form the main focus of the paper.

*Hausa Society: The Social Context*

Hausas occupy most parts of present day Northern Nigeria and the Southern Niger Republic, and part of Northern Cameroon, in addition to the Hausa communities found in many African countries, such as Ghana, Sudan, Senegal, Mali and the Gambia. Hausas are estimated to be the largest ethnic group in the whole of Africa, with a population of between 50 and 60 million (Furniss, 1996; Callaway and Creevey, 1994). The group also constitutes the largest Muslim population in Africa (Callaway and

Creevey, 1994). Islam has had a profound impact on Hausa society and this is attributed to the Islamic Jihad Movement of the 19th century, which led to the establishment of an Islamic state, the Sokoto Caliphate. The impact of the caliphate is still so profound that, by the end of 2001, most of the States that make up of the former caliphate have established *shariah* as an alternative legal system to the existing Federal secular one.

Another impact of Islam on Hausa society is the practice of seclusion[2]; that is, the system of *purdah*, by which women are expected to conduct their activities within the home, with minimal contact with the public arena. According to Longhurst (1982), virtually all Hausa Muslim families, rural or urban, practise seclusion, although the degree of the practice varies. To a large extent, the degree is determined by the income, class and level of education of the head of the family, the level of education of the woman, the type of community, (urban or rural), and, in rural areas, whether the residence is in a nucleated or dispersed settlement. The practice of seclusion has affected the nature of marital relationships. Seclusion is based on the premise that the husband provides for the material needs of his wife/wives and children. In return, the wives have to be obedient to their husbands and be secluded at home, where no man has access to them without his permission. Failure, from either side, could be grounds

---

[2] There are two categories of secluded women. The first are those who practise the extreme form of seclusion, in which women are hardly allowed to go out. If such a woman has some private issues to attend to, she sends a representative. This type of seclusion is associated with the royal families. The second category is the more widely practised one and is moderate in nature. Under this practice, a woman may go out during the night and she is also allowed to go out in the daytime for specific reasons, such as for health and education. My respondents were drawn from both these categories of women.

enough for divorce; and, since divorce carries no stigma and both men and women are expected to re-marry after divorce, there is little incentive for women to stay in a bad marriage.

Thus seclusion is part of the bargaining process between husband and wife. Imam (1993) notes this relationship between seclusion and maintenance by the husband and concludes that seclusion and domestic work are the price wives pay for maintenance by their husbands. She further said that, although a husband has the authority to seclude his wife, this is tempered by a notion of bargaining, with the husband providing maintenance and the wife obeying his authority. Marital relationships that are based on the above reciprocal exchange, rather than on joint action, will definitely affect the nature of ownership and the allocation of resources between husband and wife. In Hausa society, there is a clear demarcation between the resources of the wife and the husband within the household.

Another implication of the practice of seclusion is the creation of two separate and independent spaces for the sexes. It is a major means of establishing and maintaining gender identity. As seclusion restricts women to the private sphere and denies them access to public space, so men are also denied access to the spatial world of the secluded women in the home (Pittin, 1987; Callaway, 1987). For instance, male members of the family normally receive their visitors at the entrance or outside, in front of the house. Similarly, Pittin (1987) notes that men often feel uncomfortable in the women's section of even their own family or marital compound. Accordingly, Jackson (1981) observes that the exclusion of women from the public sphere, far from reinforcing the solidarity of men, has become a serious challenge to male dominance by developing female solidarity and independence.

The implication of the separate world for both men and women is that the control men can assert over women is limited and ineffective, since they are not always around to assert it. According to Callaway and Creevey (1994, p. 35), because there is little contact in day-to-day life between men and women, male authority is actually remote.

Another implication of the separate worlds of male and female is that it enables the women to see themselves as separate, different and independent of men. Consequently, women take decisions about production, income and social relations separately and independently of their husbands, and so women have a great deal of autonomy and power within their own world. Home provides " ... spatial reality to the women's economy and the world of women's social relations" (Jackson, 1981, p. 229).

Seclusion and other social practices, such as polygyny, have created a separate female economy in Hausa society; an economy that women develop, dominate and control Roberts (1989, p. 41). Furthermore, in a study of a Hausa village, Barkow (1972, p. 328) argues that " ... the adoption of wife seclusion has increased the extent of the local cash economy".

Since secluded women are in seclusion, how do they participate in their economic activities? Children provide them with the link to the outside world. Children, especially girls, are used by secluded women to buy raw materials from the market and to sell the goods produced. Other intermediaries used by secluded women are old women or *dilalai*, who sell the produce of the respondents for a commission. There are also women who get the raw materials of their occupation, such as rice and ground-nuts, on credit from dealers. After processing and selling the product, the money for the raw materials is paid to the dealer and another bag is taken. The women retain any profit or loss realised. The dealers are usually men; as a result, grown-up children, husbands or old women act as intermediaries.

In their social interactions, the secluded women develop and maintain their own social contacts and networks, independently of their husbands (Jackson, 1981; Pittin, 1987; Barkow, 1972). According to Pittin (1987, p. 39), " ... women's and men's time and social activities, and much of their income, are vested in same-sex networks, generally favouring their kin". Writing of these networks, Cooper (1997, p. 152) writes, " ... *zumunci*, or "kinship and friendship", is not simply blood relations; it is a feeling of closeness and mutual support, created and nurtured through numerous visits, gift exchanges, and through occasional emergency support".

It is within this context that the majority of Hausa women operate. We shall now examine how these gender relations help in shaping power relations and negotiation between husband and wife.

*Gender Relations and Women's Power*

There is little alternative to marriage for both men and women in Hausa society (Barkow, 1972; Callaway, 1984; Salamone, 1976; Solivetti, 1994). Whilst the social pressure to remain married is similar for both women and men, there is no stigma attached to divorce. Women do easily walk out of a marriage that they are not satisfied with. The frequency of divorce enables women to be in and out of marriage and therefore less dependent on marriage than men. According to Callaway (1984, p. 439) marriage for women in Hausa society is " ... a necessary social state, not a source of nurturing of emotional security". However, it is a different picture for the men. In a study of a Hausa village, Barkow (1972, p. 324) contends that " ... every man fears being left wifeless, being a comical figure whose wife has deserted him and who has failed to find another". Thus, marriage is to women an important bargaining power against men.

Despite the near universal status of marriage in Hausa society, marriage is viewed as a contract between husbands and wives, with the husband providing the material needs and the wife remaining secluded and obedient. Hausa secluded women have generally upheld and actively supported this contractual model of marriage. Whilst this action of the women may support the illusion of Hausa women's complete dependency on their husbands, it nonetheless offers advantages to women. By upholding the contractual model, the women have rendered the institution of marriage flexible and subjected it to manipulation. They can easily get out of an undesirable relationship with "flimsy" excuses, as the raw court data in Table 1 indicates. When the court failed to grant their wishes, the women "voted with their feet" by running away from the husband's house. This is called *yaji*. The main reason why men go to court is to seek for the return of their wives from *yaji*. The women can employ delaying tactics to stretch the duration of their *yaji*. In the court, I met an instance of this, in which the wife had been delaying her return to her husband for a year. When she realised that the judge's patience was running out, she agreed to return, but then raised the question of repayment for her maintenance during her stay away from his house. The argument was that, if he was still claiming his "marriage", then he should repay her maintenance expenses as required of a husband. The man was quoted a huge amount and they were negotiating the amount at the time I met them in the court.

Table 1

Women's Reasons for Going to Court

| Reasons | Total |
|---|---|
| Maintenance/payment | 1036 (54%) |
| Maltreatment | 356 (19%) |
| Confirmation of divorce | 127 (7%) |
| Allegation of adultery | 113 (6%) |
| Sex related | 95 (5%) |
| Abandonment | 47 (2%) |
| Emotional reasons | 44 (2%) |
| Sickness | 38 (2%) |
| Religious | 38 (2%) |
| Others | 41 (2%) |
| Total | 1913 (100%) |

Source: Upper Area Courts of Sokoto and Kware, 1998

In considering the contractual nature of marriage, the Hausa women have generally insisted upon the husband's role of providing food, clothing and other basic needs for the women. This has enabled them to own and accumulate their own resources. The contractual nature of marital relations has also led to a clear demarcation of resources between a wife and a husband. A wife cannot make a direct claim to the income or assets of her husband and, in the same way, the husband cannot make a claim to those of his wife (Pittin, 1987). Hill (1972, p. 27) observes that the personal relationship between husband and wife plays very little part in their economic transactions. She writes:

"A woman who makes ground-nut oil for sale is in business on her own account and there is nothing immodest about buying ground-nuts from her husband at the market price, or buying oil from herself with her 'housekeeping' money". Similarly, Schildkrout (1983, p. 114-115) notes that:

> When women cook food for sale rather than for domestic consumption, or when they engage in other income-producing activities, all their income is their own. The entire activity is distinct from their obligation to prepare food for their families .... Some women, in other words, as wives, buy food from themselves, as food-sellers, to feed their families.

Apart from the contractual nature of marriage, seclusion has also been used as an instrument of negotiation by the secluded women. First of all, the widespread nature of the practice in the early 20th century in Hausa society was linked to the rational choice women made, to be in seclusion rather than be involved in farming and the collection of energy and water. In our research, the majority of the secluded women in the rural areas have defined seclusion in relation to not engaging in farming, fetching water and gathering firewood. Thus, seclusion is a means of getting out of the harsh reality of rural life in terms of farming and water and energy collection. Secondly, and equally relevant, is the role of women in making seclusion flexible through the system of *biki*, which is meant to maintain *zumunci*, an investment in friendship, kinship and social ties. As a proverb expresses it, *"zumunta a kafa take"*; that is, *"zumunci* 'goes on foot'" (translation from Cooper, 1997, p. 153). The women are always, although most of the time at night, visiting relatives, friends, and attending ceremonies (which could involve travelling to another area and coming out in the daytime). Pittin (1988, p. 39) states that:

> It is ironic that, because of seclusion, women are seen as the immobile and constant residents of a household. In fact, women are the real migrants in Hausa society, signalling every change in marital status or career choice by physical movements, from family home to marital home, to family home, to new marital home, and so on.

Furthermore, Jackson (1981, p. 224) also observes that " ... at no time of year are women said to be immobilised within the compound". Drawing from her data, she argues that, from the figures on wedding attendance and visiting, seclusion does not really impinge on a woman's social life.

Another important source of power for women is sex. Almost all of the women cited the use of sex to influence their husband's agreement on significant issues. In the discussion of how wives get their husbands to succumb to their wishes, one woman said, "A woman knows her way. It is through satisfying him". When probed further, she hesitantly continued, "I will not allow us to have eye contact and I would refuse him what I normally give him in the night. From there he will understand and seek for compromise". In another group interview, a woman said, "With her thing (meaning sex), the best way to show your anger over his decision is to refuse yourself and he will come down over his decision".

However, the same conjugal contract that empowers the women was also used as the basis for their subordination. The burden of maintenance is viewed as the basis for a husband's authority over his wife, as noted by an elderly woman:

## "My Wife's Tongue ... "

> Your feeding is on his shoulder, all your needs are on his shoulder. If you obey marital rules, you put your parents in paradise; but if you become angry with him, don't think you gain anything, it is Satan. Satan was created for hell. Anytime your husband is angry with you, seek for his forgiveness; that day your mother and father will sleep in heaven. Every woman in this world is created in heaven, but before the sun sets in, the majority are out and into hell. It is the fault of the women. A man buys you cloth, buys you shoes; if you request for henna he buys. You do nothing but put in seclusion.

There are local tales narrating the punishment wives, (and sometimes their mothers, who connived with their daughters), received for daring to disobey and challenge the authority of their husbands. The subservient relationship expected between husband and wife was captured in my interview with an elderly woman, who explained how she settles conflicts between husband and wife.

> I then asked her to seek for his forgiveness, because Allah demands women to seek for their husband's forgiveness; but men are not required to seek their wives' forgiveness, because that will condemn a wife to hell. If she seeks his forgiveness, she goes to heaven.
>
> *Question:* If that is the way a woman goes to heaven, how does a man attain heaven?
>
> *Answer:* Through his mother and meeting the responsibility entailed in marriage.
>
> *Question:* What other ways can a woman attain heaven?

*Answer:* Through her husband.

*Question:* Can a woman attain heaven through her mother as well?

*Answer:* I swear it is the daughter who determines whether her parents go to heaven or hell by her behaviour towards her husband. If she relates well with him, the reward of that behaviour would take the parents to heaven.

Our interest here is not the authenticity or otherwise of the view, but how such a view is used to control women's rebellion. In order to achieve compliance from women, the consequences of their rebellion are extended to their parents. One of the tales tells of how a mother is put in hell for the sin of her daughter, who has run away from her husband's house.

Despite the pressures on wives to be subservient to their husbands, Hausa women, in their capacity as agents, have devised strategies to negotiate, challenge and resist their subordination. It is this ability of Hausa women to resist and subvert men's authority that we turn to next.

*Women's Resistance*

Crucial to the understanding of power relationships between wife and husband in Hausa society is the recognition that the sources and exercise of power and resistance are located and played within the context of the "rules of the game" that define the marital contract. According to Kandiyoti (1998, p. 142), " ... both the powerful and the dominated are, up to a point, bound by the same normative constraints". Hence, women's rational choices and strategies of resistance are constrained by the social context in which they operate. These strategies may involve not only the use of resources available to women, but also socially constructed meanings and definitions.

Consequently, the Hausa women use the maintenance and sex marital bargain to challenge and subvert men's authority. We shall begin with the maintenance.

*Maintenance as an Instrument of Women's Resistance*

The role of secluded women as agents in the politics of household production and consumption has been noted in the literature. Callaway (1987, p. 76) argues that, while the practice of wife seclusion is based on the premise that women are dependent consumers, women are in fact independent producers, who generate income of their own by diverting cash provided by men for domestic maintenance into production. Similarly, Schildkrout (1983) argues that, by taking resources that husbands give them for consumption and diverting them into a remunerated female sphere of production, the women are in effect receiving payment for their domestic labour. Although the socially acceptable practice of women diverting money and other food ingredients meant for household use to their food business may decrease because of the current Nigerian economic crisis, similar deception to subvert men's economic dominance is still rampant.

During our fieldwork, we observed many cases of deception and subversion by the women against their husbands and two such cases are presented below.

*Case 1: Women's Subversion of Men's Economic Dominance (1)*

One of the cases was that of a woman who bought a decorative bed sheet from her female friend and paid for it, but then requested her husband to buy it for her. The husband agreed to buy it on credit, as he did not have the money then. She told him she would contact the owner and a day later she informed him that the woman had agreed. She was expecting her husband to pay for the bed-sheet in a month's time, which would lead to a refund of her own money. If he did not pay, she would get her friend to send a child to him to remind him of the credit, which she hoped would pressurise him to pay.

*Case 2: Women's Subversion of Men's Economic Dominance (2)*

Another example was when I observed a woman sending a girl to collect money for locust beans (a soup ingredient) from her husband, who was outside the house, probably within the neighbourhood. The girl came back, saying that the husband said he did not have any money. She sent the girl back to tell him that she, the wife, also did not have any money, but that she was sending her, the girl, to a neighbour's house to get it on credit. Meanwhile, she had already bought the beans; in fact, I was waiting for her to finish pounding the beans so that I could interview her. When I raised the matter with her, she confirmed that my interpretation was right, saying that, if men know that women have money, they would not pay for many things, but would expect their wives to pay.

As previously mentioned, a fundamental component of the marital contract is maintenance. A husband has authority over his wife if he is able to fulfil his own side of the bargain - maintenance. The equating of the maintenance of the wife with men's authority means that the husband's authority over his wife is dependent on her judgement. That is, the husband has authority as long as the wife is satisfied. Thus, even if maintenance is a source of power for men, it can also be used by women to undermine such power through accusations of lack of maintenance. Similarly, lack of maintenance amounts to failure on the part of the husband, which the wife can use to ridicule and challenge her husband. Accordingly, Hill (1972, p. 151) notes that " ... one of the particular problems that beset poor men is a pronounced inability to remain married to their wives, who commonly seek divorces on the grounds of their husbands' poverty". A woman who wants to get out of a marriage can easily do so, citing lack of feeding, clothing or shelter. For instance, in the court data in Table 1, about 54% of the cases brought to court by women are maintenance-related.

*Sex as an Instrument of Women's Resistance*

As well as maintenance, sex is the other fundamental component of the marital contract; consequently, it is an important bargaining factor between husband and wife. The direct link made between being a man and the ability to satisfy a wife sexually has rendered the men vulnerable to women. Consequently, wives challenge their husbands' authority by attacking men via their symbols of power; e.g. sex. According to Salamone (1976), being a man involves being sexually satisfying to a woman, defending her from outsiders and being able to keep her. Consequently, the wife may often in a conflict challenge the sexual prowess of her husband, to get him to submit. This is best illustrated by a quotation from Salamone (1976, p. 360). It reads: "If manliness is equated with dominance, then manliness in a sexual sense can be challenged through accusation of impotence or poor sexual performance, which in turn challenges the entire structure of male dominance as a cultural ideology".

Thus, challenging their husband's manliness through accusations of impotence and poor sexual performance are amongst the strategies that Hausa wives adopt to undermine their husbands' authority. The challenge can be public, as the court data in Table 1 indicates. Of the total of 1913 cases brought by women to the court, 208 (representing 11%) were sex related. Sex can be employed by a wife to ridicule her husband in order to end a marriage, as well as to negotiate, as the case below shows.

*Case 3: Negotiation Over Sex*

A wife brought a complaint to the court against her husband, saying that he was making so many sexual demands on her that she could no longer endure it. When the man was summoned before the court, he confirmed his wife's claims. Neither partner wanted the dissolution of the marriage and therefore the judge had to intercede between them. The judge asked the wife to state the maximum number of times that she could endure having sex in a day. She cited once daily. The husband was asked whether or not this was acceptable to him. He rejected the wife's offer, but agreed to accept a reduction from ten to seven times daily. After two weeks of negotiation in the court, the couple reached a consensus of a maximum of four times daily.

*Techniques Employed in the Resistance*

According to Salamone (1976), relationships between wives and husbands in Hausa society are marked by bargaining for power, which takes place in public. The use of the public arena is strategically important for the women; for, while a man may initiate an argument, he will not carry it into the public arena, for by doing so he admits his inability to control his wife. However, women always initiate a public conjugal conflict situation in order to attract and win the public to their cause (Salamone 1976). This transfer of private conjugal conflict to the public arena may take different dimensions. Salamone (1976, p. 363) explores the use of proverbs and argues that, because proverbs capture shared attitudes towards common experiences, the women resort to attack through that channel. For instance, he cited a pregnant wife exaggerating the size of her stomach and begging her husband to prove his masculinity by beating her there, thereby " ... posing her femininity against his maleness". He argues that the heart of a woman's attack is " ... on her husband's maleness, or his power. Thus, she, made bolder by the protection afforded by the audience's presence, will choose those proverbs that will cause him to lose face". This is indeed a powerful tool, as some of Salamone's informants narrated (" ... a woman's tongue is her weapon") and as the title of this paper indicates.

Another dimension to the public display by wives is more overt and involves carrying an open confrontation and quarrel with husbands to the public to judge. This enables the wife to gain public support and thereby compels the husband into concession. The scene witnessed and narrated by Cooper (1997, pp. 22-23) in her study of the Hausa society of Maradi in the Niger Republic provides a good example of the use of the public to gain sympathy.

*Case 4: The Use of a Public Audience*

> I went down to Maradawa, to see Buga. Just as I arrived, a voluble argument erupted, attracting a large number of neighbourhood women and children .... According to Buga, the young woman who is her neighbour had just sent her husband to get her younger brother out of the hospital ... and had given her husband 550 CFA to pay the outstanding medical bill. She later discovered that she had not owed any money at all and that her husband had secretly spent the money on something else. The old woman screaming into the doorway was the young woman's mother, who was roundly abusing her son-in-law, while making public the event, her

witnessing of the transaction, and the failure of her daughter's husband to return the money.

The daughter was crying and noisily stacking her pots and pans in the courtyard, signalling her intention to leave her husband. The clatter brought the son-in-law out of the room to defend himself publicly, saying the whole thing was a lie and he never had the money....The son-in-law, silenced, slunk off with his prayer beads. When he was gone, his wife ... remarked that she was not going to run off after all ... he would just have to divorce her himself. Neighbours urged patience and offered sympathy.... Little by little, things calmed down, people went off to do their own work, and the wife sat disconsolately on a broken stool nursing her baby. Her husband crept back in to carry off his *fura;* neither of them looked at one another or spoke.

*Yaji* is one of the public expressions of overt techniques by women. *Yaji* is a Hausa name for a hot pepper. It signifies that either the issue or the whole marriage is too "hot" for the woman and she therefore needs to be cooled down. *Yaji* involves a woman running to her parents' or her relatives' home, without the knowledge of the husband. This action necessitates the husband finding out where she is and then going or sending his representative to negotiate with her and her relatives over her return. At this level, the husband has to compromise his position on the issue of discord if he wants her back, thereby putting pressure on him to reach a consensus.

However, Barkow (1972, p. 322) sees *yaji* as a powerful tool, because:

> Without his wife, a man must either bear the enormous shame of cooking his own food, or the lesser shame of asking a friend or kinswoman to provide for him. In order to get her, his wife, to return, a man must go humbly to his in-laws, with whom he has the strongest of shame-avoidance relationships, and beg for her ...

"My Wife's Tongue ... "

he inevitably suffers considerable shame and embarrassment in the process.

The cases presented so far indicate the strategic use of the public arena by the women in relation to male power. Whilst a man loses face if he makes conjugal conflict public, the wife does it to gain public support against her husband, particularly if she has been wronged. The transfer of conjugal conflict to the public arena by the wife may also compel the husband to make concessions over his position on an issue. A wife may also use the public audience to ridicule and shame her husband through the use of proverbs and tales. The technique of using a public audience in a conjugal conflict may prevent bodily injuries, as the public audience are expected to intercede; as Salamone (1976, p. 361) notes, " ... when conflict takes place in public, it will not be allowed by the audience to become violent or to last an undue length of time".

*Conclusion*

The quotation in the title of this paper is indicative of the power of women in a patriarchal Hausa society. It also implies some element of bargaining between husband and wife. Equally important is the fact that the quotation is a summation of men's views of women's power and resistance. Women's verbal tools were deemed to be more effective in punishing and challenging husbands who wrong their wives than Ali's punches.

*References*

Allen, A. (1999). *The power of feminist theory:*

*Domination, resistance, solidarity.* Boulder, CO: Westview.

Barkow, J. H. (1972). Hausa women and Islam. *Canadian Journal of African Studies, 6* (2), 317-328.

Callaway, B. J. (1987). *Muslim Hausa women in Nigeria: Tradition and change.* Syracuse, NY: Syracuse University Press.

Callaway, B. J. (1984). Ambiguous consequences of socialisation of Hausa women. *Modern African Studies, 22* (3), 429-450.

Callaway, B. J., & Creevey, L. (1994). *The heritage of Islam: Women, religion and politics in West Africa.* Boulder, CO: Lynne Rienner.

Cooper, B. M. (1997). *Marriage in Maradi: Gender and culture in a Hausa society in Niger, 1900-1989.* Oxford: James Currey.

Furniss, G. (1996). *Poetry, prose and popular culture in Hausa.* Edinburgh: Edinburgh University Press, for the International African Institute.

Hill, P. (1972). *Rural Hausa: A village and a setting.* London: Cambridge University Press.

Imam, A. M. (1993). *If you won't do these things for me, I won't do seclusion for you: Local and regional constructions* of seclusion ideologies and practices in Kano, Northern Nigeria. Unpublished doctoral dissertation, University of Sussex.

Jackson, C. (1981). *Change and rural Hausa women: A study in Kura and Rano districts, Northern Nigeria.* Unpublished doctoral dissertation, University of London.

Kandiyoti, D. (1998). Gender, power and contestation. In R. Pearson, & C. Jackson, (Eds.), *Feminist visions of development: Gender, analysis and policy* (pp 135-151). London: Routledge.

Longhurst, R. (1982). Resource allocation and the sexual division of labour: Case study of a Muslim Hausa village. In L. Beneria (Ed.), *Women and development: the sexual division of labor in rural societies* (pp. 95-115). New York: Praeger.

Moore, H. L. (1994). *A passion for difference: Essays in anthropology and gender.* Cambridge: Polity Press.

Pittin, R. (1987). Documentation of women's work in Nigeria. In C. Oppong (Ed.), *Sex roles, population and development in West Africa: Policy-related studies on work and demographic issues* (pp. 25-44). Portsmouth, NH: Heinemann.

Pittin, R. (1988). Social status and economic opportunity in urban Hausa society. In F. A. Ogunsheye, C. Di Domenico, K. Awosika and O. Akinkoye (Eds.), *Nigerian women and development* (pp. 264-279). Ibadan: Ibadan University Press.

Roberts, P. (1989). The sexual politics of labour in Western Nigeria and Hausa Niger. In K. Young (Ed.), *Serving two masters: Third World women in development* (pp. 27-48). Ahmedabad: Allied Publishers.

Salamone, F. A. (1976). The arrow and the bird: Proverbs in the solution of Hausa conjugal conflict. *Journal of Anthropological Research, 32,* 358-371.

Schildkrout, E. (1983). Dependency and autonomy: The economic activities of secluded Hausa women in Kano. In C. Oppong (Ed.), *Female and male in West Africa* (pp. 107-126). London: Allen & Unwin.

Solivetti, L. M. (1994). Family, marriage and divorce in a Hausa community: A sociological model. *Africa, 64* (2), 253-271.

*Additional Reading*

Bryceson, D. (1995). Gender relations in rural Tanzania: Power politics or cultural consensus? In C. Creighton & C. K. Omari (Eds.), *Gender, family and household in*

*Tanzania* (pp. 37-69). Aldershot: Avebury.

Coles, C. (1991). Hausa women's work in a declining urban economy: Kaduna, Nigeria, 1980-1985. In C. Coles & B. Mack (Eds.), *Hausa women in the twentieth century* (pp. 163-192). Madison, WI: University of Wisconsin Press.

Cooper, B. M. (1998). Gender and religion in Hausaland: variations in Islamic practice in Niger and Nigeria. In H. L. Bodman & N. Tohidi (Eds.), *Women in Muslim societies: Diversity within unity* (pp. 21-37). Boulder, CO: Lynne Rienner.

Hill, P. (1977). *Population, prosperity and poverty: Rural Kano, 1900 and 1970.* Cambridge: Cambridge University Press.

Imam, A. (1991). The development of women's seclusion in Hausaland, Northern Nigeria. In *Women living under Muslim laws, dossier 9/10,* (pp. 4-18). Grabels: Women Living Under Muslim Laws.

Knipp, M. (1987). *Women, Western education and change: A case study of the Hausa-Fulani of Northern Nigeria.* Unpublished doctoral dissertation, North Western University.

Mack, B. (1991). Royal wives in Kano. In C. Coles and B. Mack (Eds.), *Hausa women in the twentieth century* (pp. 109-130). Madison, WI: University of Wisconsin Press.

Pittin, R. (1989). *Women, work and ideology in a context of economic crisis: A Nigerian case study.* The Hague: Institute of Social Studies.

Simmons, E. B. (1976). *Economic research on women in rural development in Northern Nigeria.* Washington, DC: American Council on Education, Overseas Liaison Committee.

Smith, M. F. (1981). *Baba of Karo: A woman of the Muslim Hausa.* (New ed.) New Haven, CT: Yale University Press.

# 4

# A SHORT HISTORY OF NATURE: FEMINISM AND TRANSCENDENTAL PHYSIOLOGY

## Jill Marsden

The history of Western feminist thinking has been marked by the strength of its resistance to the ideology of biological determinism. Challenging the view that certain social roles are naturally ordained or biologically inevitable continues to be politically vital in an epoch that privileges the "findings" of scientific research as value-neutral, impartial and beyond dispute. These critiques notwithstanding, the humanistic prejudice that culture defines itself in its transcendence of nature has led many feminist theorists into a conceptual impasse. Thus, despite astute deconstruction of the discourses that naturalise and legitimate social inequities, the so-called "facts" of female embodiment have seemed impossible to theorise away. As Sherry B. Ortner (1974) has remarked: "Because of woman's greater bodily involvement with the natural functions surrounding reproduction, she is seen as more a part of nature than man is" (p. 76). Human existence, as either male or female, would seem to be an incontrovertible fact of biological difference; a fact that remains essential after all arguments concerning the restrictive ideology surrounding "natural processes" have been voiced. Whatever feminists may have to say about the way in which the female body is socially coded and inscribed, there are basic facts that make a female "female". Surely there are *material limits* to what can be reinvented?

It is the very *nature* of this self-evident truth that will be questioned in the following discussion. Firstly, some of the ways in which the concept of nature has been employed in "second wave" feminist thinking will be explored, focusing on an analysis of the female body in particular. It will then be asked how these ideas address the questions of what it is to have and to live a sexed body and whether or not the concept of a "true sex" is a useful one. Finally, the discussion will consider what it would mean for feminist practice to develop an approach to nature that acknowledges *the reality of ideas*. For reasons that will be subsequently explained, this approach will be called "transcendental physiology".

## 1. *The Nature that is Nurtured*

It seems that there are few "facts" about sex and gender that have not been called into question in the course of several decades of feminist scholarship. It has been an abiding goal of feminism to challenge and resist the conflation of biological and social identities and to expose the ways in which prevailing ideologies produce normative models of "sex appropriate" behaviour *as natural*. The elision of the distinction between maternity as a medical and as a social category perhaps remains the most striking example of this naturalisation. The argument that women are physiologically destined to "nurture" (and hence should be socialised accordingly) is an ideological construction that has long been used to discriminate against females seeking to succeed in a male-dominated market-place, although the popularity enjoyed by the "maternal deprivation" thesis ebbs and flows in line with the need for female workers (Pascall, 1997, p. 77-78). Marking a clear distinction between the concepts of "sex" as a biological "given" and "gender" as its cultural interpretation has thus been an invaluable tool in undermining the determinist arguments that maintain that certain inequalities are naturally generated, not socially fuelled. To this end, feminists have taken issue with the claim that certain hormones or physiological traits predispose certain behaviours and have repeatedly argued against the notion that features of a social world (such as a caring, domestic role or an aggressive or predatory manner) are biologically driven and a-historical (Smart, 1996). Indeed, feminist contributions to the nature-nurture debate have strongly emphasised the role which socialisation plays in the process of gender acquisition, downplaying the role of "nature" accordingly. Given the academic respectability enjoyed by sociobiological works that seek to establish the "inevitability of patriarchy" (e.g. Goldberg, 1974), this work remains essential.

However, in spite of this well-defined approach to the interpretation of biological sex differences, the concept of "nature" has continued to represent a site of unease for feminist thinkers. To insist that the physiologically specific experiences of men and women are *merely* the result of cultural perceptions gives far too much weight to the "social". For example, it would be facile to claim that gender identity is so fluid a category that it can be revised at will or that menstruation and pregnancy are simply cultural "constructions". In fact, since it has been politically important for feminism to emphasise those *material* differences that segment and divide people from one another, feminist thinkers have often found themselves charged with a kind of gender essentialism even when seeking to make "constructionist" claims. Quite simply, it *matters* that women's bodies appear to equip them for child-bearing or appear to mark them out as targets for discrimination, harassment or assault. The word "appear" is used advisedly here, for these *are* "perceptions"; but many would want to insist that they are produced by empirically real experience. In other words, the signifiers of gender may shift (and be "reinvented"), but the nature to which they ultimately refer does not. In short, in challenging patriarchal determinations of male and female bodies, it would seem that feminist thinking is obliged to offer an alternative model of the "truth" of what it is to be a man or a woman, thereby replacing one fundamentalist model of nature with another.

One option for feminist thinking at this juncture is to reject the patriarchal determinations of female nature that one finds unacceptable, demeaning and prejudicial, postponing the question of the "truth" of female embodiment as such. The problem with this approach is that it begs the question of how one can distinguish the interpretation that is deemed sexist from the given *reality* of nature. Unless one is prepared to regard sexual reproduction as a cultural perception, the biological differences between males and females have to be addressed. Thwarted in her interesting attempts to do the former, Simone de Beauvoir, in *The Second Sex* (1972, p. 63), concludes that, since woman is held in "the iron grasp of the species" and biologically "destined" for the repetition of life, it is female nature, as such, that must be refused. Despite equivocation on this issue, Beauvoir is unable to shake off the suspicion that the truth of woman's social subordination may stem from an ultimately irrefutable physiological weakness. Accordingly, she attributes to the female body a troubling infirmity that persists despite the most laudable efforts to transcend one's facticity:

> The conflict between species and individual, which sometimes assumes dramatic force at childbirth, endows the female body with a disturbing frailty. It has been well said that women "have infirmity in the abdomen"; and it is true that they have within them

a hostile element - it is the species gnawing at their vitals.

(Beauvoir, 1972, p. 63)

True existentialist freedom is only possible for woman, Beauvoir argues, if she succeeds in rising above her biological facticity; in other words, if she rejects maternity as a potential "project". Taking this argument a stage further, Shulamith Firestone argues in *The Dialectic of Sex* (1979) that a sexual revolution can only be consequent upon a biological revolution and hence that only through reproduction, *ex utero*, will women gain genuine sexual equality: "Nature produced the fundamental inequality - half the human race must bear and rear the children of all of them" (p. 192). Firestone claims: "To free women from their biology would be to threaten the *social* unit that is organized around biological reproduction and the subjection of women to their biological destiny, the family" (pp. 193-4). Attempting to reform the social organisation of biology is dismissed as almost entirely worthless: "Day care centres buy women off. They ease the immediate pressure without asking why that pressure is on *women*" (p. 193).

Notoriously, Firestone looked to innovations in ectogenic reproductive technology to liberate women from the pregnancies she deemed "barbaric". Many of Firestone's readers have been wary of such unrestrained appeals to technology in the context of women's liberation. Radical feminists have highlighted the ways in which new reproductive technologies, such as *in vitro* fertilization, are motivated by commercial and professional objectives, how amniocentesis may be used to pre-select female foetuses for abortion, and how sterilization and hazardous contraceptive experiments have been particularly targeted at coloured women (Wajcman, 1991). Moreover, they have been quick to point out that gender relations have profoundly influenced the form that technological advances have taken: for example, it is routinely *women's* bodies that are subject to scrutiny and manipulation when fertility problems arise. In short, the tacit codification of culture as "male" and nature as "female" has had profound repercussions on the way in which any appeal to technology is interpreted. Nature is seen as a *resource* that is "acted on" and manipulated for cultural endeavour; and it is man (in the non-generic sense of the term) who is alone free to assert himself "artificially" through science, technology and art. Indeed, the subsumption of matter to form, via the ongoing march of reason, is a story that Western thinkers have fondly repeated to themselves as the essence of history itself. It is scarcely fortuitous that, in his account of the generation of things, Plato (trans. 1937) should gender the imposition of form upon elemental matter in terms of male procreation and female receptivity (*Timaeus*, 50b-51a ff.) Indeed, one could chart a history of narratives from Aristotle to Marx that persist with a hylomorphic model of matter, in which a paternal, despotic or divine agency systematically keeps nature down.

This may, in part, explain why the chief resistance to Firestone's recommendations has been based on arguments that organised post-biological reproduction is *unnatural*. From such a humanist perspective, technology is regarded as the contrary of nature rather than one aspect of its broader material development. The notion of the organic integrity of the body - which we tamper with at our peril - is perhaps the most overt theological prejudice subtending these debates. However, it is worth pointing out that Firestone's arguments actually work to reinforce rather than to challenge this notion of a divine order of things. This is exemplified by her understanding of sexual difference in terms of a "fundamental inequality" that is written into nature, requiring a literal transcendence of the body. Her exotic recommendations for biological revolution belie a strangely patriarchal evaluation of the maternal. Needless to say, there is no negotiation here with those who view motherhood as a positive "life choice". This is not to deny that an unequivocal celebration of the maternal - as a positive sign of a specifically female identity - runs the risk of reinscribing the very biological determinism that an emphasis on the social construction of gender roles sought to displace. Skewing the political argument away from corporeality in an attempt to deflect this charge may do little more than subtly reinstate patriarchal ideology, as attempts to develop a feminist ethic of "care" demonstrate (Segal, 2000, p. 34). Either women are regarded as differently situated moral agents (owing to their greater involvement in domesticity and child rearing) or else they are corporeally neutral moral agents, modelled on a masculinist paradigm of the universal subject. Whether one seeks to transcend or to affirm feminine matter, it would seem that the *nature of female nature* remains extrinsic to interpretation.

The question that imposes itself here concerns what the possession of a particular body prohibits or makes possible. The tendency to "sex" bodies according to reproductive capacity may say more about a dominant capitalist economy than any given biological reality. Arguably, the changing nature of the "workplace" and the sexual division of labour, coupled with advances in reproductive technology, may contribute to a progressive re-evaluation of the maternal role. However, even if one were to "transcend" the fact that one possesses a womb, it might be argued that other "facts" of female embodiment are not so easily subverted. For example, in *Against Our Will: Men, Women and Rape* (1975), Susan Brownmiller argues: "Man's structural capacity to rape and woman's corresponding structural vulnerability are as basic to the physiology of both our sexes as the primal act of sex itself" (p. 14). She goes on to claim:

> Had it not been for this accident of biology ... there would be neither copulation nor rape as we know it. Anatomically one might want to improve on the design of nature, but such speculation appears to my mind as unrealistic ... we cannot work around the fact that in terms of human anatomy the possibility of forcible intercourse incontrovertibly exists. This single factor may have been sufficient to have caused the creation of the male ideology of rape. When men discovered that they could rape, they proceeded to do it. (Brownmiller, 1974, p. 14)

Brownmiller's argument that the ability to perform a certain act accounts for its prevalence might at first sight seem a truism, yet here, no less than with maternity, one might ask what constitutes this state of affairs as "natural". The possibility of forced intercourse does exist, but since it exists as an idea as well as an act, the question ought to be: what *allows* this to emerge as an idea upon which one *will* act? There are very many acts of violence of which the average man or woman is physically capable, but they do not need to perform them to discover this putative "fact". It is probable that there are many more of which they are capable, but which they will never encounter as ideas, simply because they have no socially relevant currency. For example, on Brownmiller's reasoning, the possession of fingers constitutes the structural capacity to jab other human beings in the eye, a possibility which "incontrovertibly exists", but suffice it to say that this idea does not *materialise* for most people as biologically inevitable. To say that rape is an event to be interpreted, rather than a biological given, is to acknowledge that the nature of aggressor and victim is constructed, not to deny that rape is real.

To claim that rape is an event to be interpreted is to acknowledge that its "truth" is materially embedded in a social framework rather than ontologically given - a point to which we shall return. This does not entail a belief that rape is metaphorical: one might argue that the very concept of metaphor implies the "truth" of the model for which it is a sign. The point is that the nature of a body is not in itself meaningful. To be "feminine" or to experience oneself as a "woman" is not *dependent* on any essential physiology, despite the fact that one's body *materially determines the way in which one thinks about oneself*. As preoperative transsexuals indicate, feeling that one *is* a "woman" or a "man" is as much a product of ideas about what constitutes a coherent gender as it is about the possession of certain organs or hormones. The desire to "reinvent" nature in this particular context suggests that it is the *idea* of nature that has a determining effect, not nature "as such". However, it is a certain idea of nature that is *lived,* and hence experienced as materially inevitable, which contours the works of Beauvoir, Firestone and Brownmiller. Each upholds a version of biological determinism that presents female inferiority and subordination as given. The challenge for a feminist philosophy of the body is to enable social interpretations of nature to materialise in ways that no longer play to a patriarchal script. The question is: how is it possible to tell a new truth about nature, without falling prey to the logic of essentialism?

## 2. *The Quest for A True Sex*

In the quest to establish how ideas about nature become socially realised, the phenomenon of gender-reassignment rewards closer scrutiny. The key feminist axiom that sex is biologically given, whereas gender is socially ascribed, is at one level undermined by the proposition that sex is also a mutable category. As has been well documented, a gender essentialism dominates the debates on transsexual identity (Raymond, 1980). The notion of being trapped in the "wrong body" implies a fundamental relationship between the physical features of sex and psychological attitude. This tends to indicate that expectations about gender-appropriate ways of life serve as the template for regarding bodies as appropriately sexed. Indeed, it is a paradox of transsexual affectivity that one's body is regarded as an inconsequential determinant of gender, yet the goal of surgery is to instantiate sex retrospectively as a causal factor. In this case, the idea of a "true nature" seems to have greater "reality" than any empirically observable "facts" about the body. In one respect, this view is echoed by Janice Raymond in her controversial text, *The Transsexual Empire* (1980), in which she argues that operations to change sex fail to address the crux of what it is to identify as feminine or masculine. However, whilst the biological fundamentalism of would-be transsexuals is presented as erroneous, Raymond appears to hold that sex remains a crucial determinant of the truth of bodies nevertheless. Alarmed by the prospect that the production of "she-males" is the ultimate act of patriarchal manipulation of femininity, she declares: "All transsexuals rape women's bodies by reducing the real female form to an artefact, appropriating this body for themselves" (p. 104). There are a number of questionable assumptions in this claim, not least that there is a "real female form" that is violated (and rendered artificial). The gap between the "reality" of women's bodies and the artifice of the transsexual is elided into a transgression which itself repeats and perpetuates the blurring of boundaries: rape. The status of rape in Raymond's account as both metaphorical and real calls into question the point that it was presumably designed to support: namely, that there is a natural extra-linguistic reality. In fact, the strange logic of this argument can only function by dematerialising sexual violence, female embodiment and transsexual experience in turn. Unanchored to the bodies that could know them, these ideas contribute towards the ideological construction of the transsexual as deviant. However, what is apparently not in dispute is the "truth" of female identity; for, interestingly, both this critique of transsexualism and the "phenomenon" thus diagnosed uphold the "natural attitude" towards gender as dichotomous and mutually exclusive.

This ideology has certainly prevailed in medical interventions to assign sex to children born with ambiguous genitalia. Closer analysis of these cases indicates that there is no clear consensus as to the authentic referent for the category "sex", since chromosome pattern and anatomy may be at odds with one another (Warnke, 2001, pp. 127-128). Since it is not clear that medical "treatment" is actually required in these cases, it would seem reasonable to assume that concern for future psychological well being is the dominating factor in sex-assignment. In other words, it is culture that insists on the necessity of nature as unequivocal, incontrovertible and transparent. This implies that, if biology determines gender, this is only because the requirements of gender have already determined that it will do so.

A famous case that has been often cited to uphold the position that gender identity owes more to rearing than to biological sex has recently been revisited. After a routine circumcision on an eight-month old boy in 1966 went disastrously wrong, a decision was made to bring the child up as a girl (Colapinto, 2000). The child's parents consulted John Money, an expert in the practice of gender-reassignment, who counselled them to enforce gender socialisation as strictly as possible. The parents withheld the fact of the early surgery from their child and Bruce - now Brenda - was encouraged to play with dolls, wear dresses and envisage a stereotypically female destiny. Psychological researchers into sex differences have often quoted this case when exploring the relation between nature and nurture and have used it as evidence of the power of the latter over the former. More recently, however, the case has been publicised because it has subsequently come to light that the child in question did not accept a feminine gender identity. The feminine toys, clothes and lifestyle were all signally rejected in favour of boys' toys, games and behaviours. After years of disruptive behaviour and underachievement at school, Brenda was told of her earlier reassignment. Hormone injections were then discontinued and, later, various operations to reconstruct a penis were attempted. Now known as David Reimer, the subject of this case lives as a married man and has adopted his wife's children.

Are we to conclude from this study that sex is innate and that nature will reassert itself, despite all attempts to instil a contrary gender identity through social learning? Brenda's twin brother, Brian, claims that his sister had no interest in housework, getting married or wearing make-up; indeed was actively hostile towards stereotypically "feminine" pursuits (Colapinto, 2000, p. 57). However, it is worth pointing out that many adolescent girls disdain these things. Indeed, feminism is in part fuelled by an impassioned resistance to the constraining aspects of the social roles reserved for women. It is also worth pointing out that Brenda was denied the flexibility in gender socialisation that many parents condone, since her family had been counselled to enforce a feminising repertoire of behaviours as strictly as possible. Perhaps the question ought to be: what prompted the decision to reassign sex in the first place? As Georgia Warnke (2001) has observed, it would seem that in this case the body is re-made to fit with the expectations of gender - our ideas about the appearance of bodies - rather than reassigning our ideas about sex and finding new ways of living out ambiguities.

In the light of the foregoing discussion, it must be acknowledged that the attempt to tell the "truth" about sex cannot be isolated from categories of validity and objectivity that are themselves cultural constructs. Debates between realism and relativism tend to be united in the assumption that there is a core reality available to inquiry. In this respect, their differences are epistemological rather than ontological. The question is whether we can adequately "know" the world or can only offer a description from a given knowledge perspective. To move on from this view and say that there are only perspectives (as social constructionist theory might sometimes be taken to imply) does not entail the conclusion that any perspective is as valid as any other, nor that gendered positions are merely shifting signifiers that can be rewritten at will. Some ideas appear to be more socially constructed than others. For example, the codification of the female body as maternal, nurturing and caring is far more culturally embedded than the view that it is an aggressive, violent or fighting body.

An objection to the latter point might be that women have a biological capacity to bear children, but that they lack the large doses of testosterone that mark them apart from their male counterparts, who are more naturally aggressive. In other words, the argument that these are social ascriptions can be challenged by the biological determinist who can adduce seemingly natural causal factors to account for these roles. But what is it that convinces us that maternity is natural, whereas violent female behaviour is less so? If sex hormones determine gender, it seems difficult to explain why any adults would ever present themselves for sex-reassignment. Moreover, as Warnke (2001, p. 132) points out, the effects of testosterone can only be identified as causal of male violence if a propensity to aggression is already interpreted as masculine. It seems that everything hinges on how the body is understood as a site of cultural production and on what is actually being said in the claim that cultural determinations "produce" bodies. If the claim is that we can never have knowledge of the way in which the body is "in itself", but only as it appears to us through the lens of a given culture, then we would be entitled to designate it a Kantian *transcendental* argument. Kant (1933) defined his philosophical task as one that concerns itself not so much with the "object" in question, but with our mode of knowing the object. In other words, we are entitled to assume that there is a "true nature" subtending experience, but we are not entitled to assume that our mental capacities are perfectly equipped to ascertain it. Kant held that human experience is limited by *a priori* forms of intuition and categories of understanding. These limiting factors also define the boundaries of our possible knowledge of the world, for they represent assumptions which have to be made about our worldly experience for it to be constituted as an item of experience *for us* at all. For example, "space" and "time" are necessary conditions of the human experience of objects. If we accept the notion that there is such an indispensable "grammar" of any particular human experience, we might be able to extend the Kantian position to account for the fact that particular bodies are "sexed" in culturally specific ways. Kant's focus was on the ideal conditions of cognition, but one might wish to argue that these features also have a history and that they might be thought of materially in terms of bodies.

Since sex is only one way of understanding bodies, it might be asked how relevant it is to an understanding of our nature as human beings. Perhaps, in the West, sex has served as imperative to our understanding of the reproduction of culture; but, if sex is a "cultural" *a priori* category, this implies that it is susceptible to change. This would mean that there *is* no core "truth" behind "appearances". Whilst Kant did not overtly relinquish the belief in noumenal reality, his insight that objects do not exist ontologically prior to the thinking that constitutes them marks the path towards such a *material* rethinking of the transcendental. As the world of work, communication and exchange is recontoured by new technologies (new material conditions), perhaps the nature of the body is being made anew.

3. *Towards a Transcendental Physiology*

In order to understand what it means to say that the body is *really* remade and not merely resignified, it is important to grasp the thought that the body is the realised product of a set of evaluations. For example, a certain corporeal identity (as weak, or powerful, or protective) is lived with such conviction that it cannot be easily reinterpreted or reassessed. One *learns* to embody a certain set of values, just as one learns to live the body of an aggressor, a survivor, even a victim. "Space" may seem to be an a-historical and "objective" framework of experience, but, if one is socialised to inhabit space in a gendered way, then it will in turn be evaluated from this perspective. For example, one makes space for the male passenger on the bus, he commands more space, more space is made for him because he commands more space, and so forth. One might make this point discursively, as Judith Butler (1993) has done: "There is no reference to a pure body which is not at the same time a further formation of that body" (p. 10). However, if one insists on thinking of the body as realised *evaluations*, the critical project takes on a further genealogical dimension. If we have learned to "incorporate" patriarchal values, the question is how to prime the body for re-evaluation.

A transcendental physiology will insist on regarding the material conditions of interpretation as the result of prior evaluations. Accordingly, this approach asks what has motivated and continues to motivate the models that we employ to make sense of our perceived reality. For example, why persist in sexing female bodies in terms of reproduction? Arguably, it is not the "biological facts" of reproduction that licence this view, but rather a question of *what conception of nature is nurtured*. It is the conceptions that girls are potential mothers, that older women are post-maternal (matronly) figures, that childlessness is a relevant social identity, which position women in terms of reproduction, whether they ever give birth or not. Within the perspective of transcendental physiology, nature is seen as both conditioned *and* conditioning. This means that nature is not a blank resource upon which different cultural interpretations might be imposed, but is simultaneously constituted by the ideas with which it is invested and "lived". Attempts made by feminists to "rewrite" the feminine body as autoerotic (Irigaray, 1985; Cixous, 1986) or as simultaneously erotic *and* maternal (Kristeva, 1986) serve to redefine the terms of the debate in which the *nature of female nature* is addressed. Whilst these works have frequently been interpreted as positivist ontologies of sexuality and have been consumed according to prevailing interpretations of the female body as the signifier of sex, it is important to emphasise that rewriting the body need not be interpreted as a merely textual gesture. In fact, in contrast to the view of female nature held by certain second wave feminists, thinkers from the "deconstructive" tradition have experimented with new modes of philosophical expression in the bid to establish new material realities. Again, if the point is grasped that bodies produce evaluations and evaluations in turn produce bodies, these innovations can be appreciated in their full materialist register and need not be commuted to the fantasies of linguistic idealism.

We might also ask: why persist in evaluating male bodies as potentially aggressive and female bodies as potentially vulnerable to this aggression? To say that this assumption reflects the sad reality of our social world merely begs the question as to why the world is seen in this way. As Sharon Marcus argues,

> [A rapist's] *belief* that he has greater strength than a woman and that he can use it to rape her merits more analysis than the putative fact of that strength, because that belief often produces as an effect the male power that appears to be rape's cause. (Marcus, 1992, p. 390)

In other words, to view the violent sexual conquest of women by men as in some sense inevitable - as Brownmiller could be taken to imply - is to foreclose the possibility that such violence can be deflected, fought and overcome.

A tactic used by guerrilla armies to outwit a seemingly greater and better-equipped military unit is to capitalise upon the element of surprise in a situation of conflict. Acting unpredictably, using knowledge of the aggressor tactically (including harnessing its strength rather than seeking to meet it head on) are ways of rewriting the rules of engagement that will favour the party presumed to be weaker. As martial artists and self-defence practitioners have usefully demonstrated, strength is as much created *in* a conflict situation as it could be said to pre-exist it. What are refused in this strategy are the terms of the debate as such (i.e. that one is already either strong or weak, either active or passive, that one must either attack or resist). In fact, if one refuses to assume that the facts of nature are given, one might be able to devise a range of strategies for resisting the determinants of culture. We can cultivate alternative accounts of nature that acknowledge that boundaries materialise in a given situation. They are not pre-given. What is proposed at a tactical level, in terms of avoidance and deflection of engagement with an aggressor, might be usefully thought about at a transcendental level. The world that we inhabit is materially composed of the ideas that we have about it. This does not mean that we can rewrite the social at will or that the body is simply the product of a theory. What it does mean is that we can acknowledge the reality of physiology in terms of what will *count* as natural in a given context, without necessarily having recourse to the assumption that one is either male or female.

*References*

Beauvoir, S. de. (1972). *The second sex* (H. M. Parshley, Trans.). Harmondsworth: Penguin. (Original work published 1949).

Brownmiller, S. (1975). *Against our will: Men, women and rape*. New York: Simon and Schuster.

Butler, J. (1993). *Bodies that matter: On the discursive limits of "sex"*. New York: Routledge.

Cixous, H. (1986). Sorties. In H. Cixous & C. Clément, *The newly born woman* (pp. 63-132) (B. Wing, Trans.). Manchester, Manchester University Press. (Original work published 1977).

Colapinto, J. (2000). *As nature made him: The boy who was raised as a girl*. New York: HarperCollins.

Firestone, S. (1979). *The dialectic of sex: The case for feminist revolution*. London: Women's Press. (Original work published 1970).

Goldberg, S. (1974). *The inevitability of patriarchy*. New York: William Morrow.

Irigaray, L. (1985). *This sex which is not one* (C. Porter, with C. Burke (Trans.). Ithaca, NY: Cornell University Press. (Original work published 1977).

Kant, I. (1933). *Critique of pure reason* (N. K. Smith, Trans.). London: Macmillan. (Original work published 1781; second edition published 1787).

Kristeva, J. (1986). Stabat mater. In T. Moi (Ed.), *The Kristeva reader*, (pp. 160-186). Oxford: Blackwell. (Original work published 1977).

Marcus, S. (1992). Fighting bodies, fighting words: A theory and politics of rape prevention. In J. Butler & J. W. Scott (Eds.),

*Feminists theorize the political,* (pp. 385-403). London: Routledge.

Ortner, S. B. (1974). Is female to male as nature is to culture? In M. Z. Rosaldo and L. Lamphere (Eds.), *Women, culture and society,* (pp. 67-87). Stanford, CA: Stanford University Press.

Pascall, G. (1997). *Social policy: A new feminist analysis.* London: Routledge.

Plato (1937). *Plato's cosmology: The "Timaeus" of Plato* (F.M. Cornford, Trans.). London: Kegan Paul.

Raymond, J. G. (1980). *The transsexual empire: The making of the she-male.* London: Women's Press.

Segal, L. (2000). Only contradictions on offer. *Women: A Cultural Review, 11* (1/2), 19-36.

Smart, C. (1996). Deconstructing motherhood. In E. B. Silva (Ed.), *Good enough mothering?: Feminist perspectives on lone motherhood,* (pp. 37-57). London: Routledge.

Wajcman, J. (1991). *Feminism confronts technology.* Cambridge: Polity Press.

Warnke, G. (2001). Intersexuality and the categories of sex. *Hypatia, 16* (3), 126-137.

5

# BECOMING GENDERED: FEMINIST BEAUTY RI(GH)TES

## Karen Stevenson

*Introduction: "One is not born, one becomes a woman"*

Long before I consciously identified myself as a feminist, I was all too aware, as are many other women, of the stringent social hierarchy that separates the beautiful from the mundane and the mundane from the "drab, ugly [and] loathsome" (Young, 1990, p. 123). As a short and bespectacled teenager, my aim was to avoid loathsomeness rather than aspire to beauty; for, despite the desire that men be "tall, dark and handsome", I was aware of the difference in the ways in which male and female attractiveness might be assessed. My brother could not stand women with flabby thighs; a male friend constantly sought reassurance from others that his girlfriend was considered beautiful; my own partner critically commented on the wobbliness of my bottom; and yet none of these men were particularly good looking themselves. While men appeared to be more autonomous, to *be* already, I was instructed, via a range of media, on how to *become*. Initially, I diligently studied the texts, but it began to seem that men's cultural security depended far less on physical appearance than did women's. Indeed, where beauty was concerned, men seemed to gain more prestige from their *female* partner's appearance than their own. It seemed that a beautiful woman functioned as a desirable commodity, to be possessed and displayed to competitors as a mirror of one's own taste, desirability and pulling power.

Academic feminism of the time also appeared to offer a biting critique of a beauty system that continued to oppress women in its idealisation of physical perfection and its capacity to seduce women into performing specific forms of femininity designed for the consumption of more powerful others (Henley, 1977; Brownmiller, 1984; Lakoff & Scherr, 1984; Chapkis, 1986). I argue that this understanding of beauty - as an oppressive imposition - incorporated a particular view of gender (and the norms associated with it) as a socially constructed debilitation imposed upon all women by virtue of their biological sex - a construct moreover that, once deconstructed, could be transcended and left behind. Dinnerstein and Weitz (1994, p. 19), for example, suggest that effective resistance to beauty is possible " ... if women become more aware of the insidious, internalized ways that the discipline of femininity disempowers women and join together to fight it".

However, the conscious attempt to develop a feminist aesthetic and reject impositional femininity was not a success. Of her own "feminist look", Susan Brownmiller says, "I hated my martyrdom" (1984, p. 57) and admits that, while she would like to fight against the double standards of appearance, she also wants to look "youthful, dazzling, feminine". It began to appear that concerns over appearance were not to be simply cast aside with a tad more willpower or " ... a little feminist rhetoric along the lines of accepting the 'real me'" (Davis, 1995, p. 55). Later feminist work on the production of the female body was more sceptical about the possibilities for transcendence (Bartky, 1990; Young, 1990; Bordo, 1993; Mama, 1995; Davis, 1995). Bartky and Bordo, for example, both began from the Foucauldian notion of the body as a site of inscription - "an object and target of power" - to argue that women were embedded within culture and could not, therefore, help but collude with it. Bartky argued that women's sense of themselves as women was dependent upon the production of a body " ... felt to be feminine" (1990, p. 77), one that fitted the expectations of our real or imagined communities. And Louise Bennet highlights the pressure exerted by archetypes of femininity:

I hate dat ironed hair

And dat bleaching skin

Hate dat ironed hair

And dat bleaching skin.

But I'll be all alone

If I don't fall in. (cited in Mama, 1995, p. 149)

More recently, then, the social hierarchies articulated by the norms of beauty and gender have been perceived as more complex; for a start, appearance has historically connoted identities of class and race, as well as gender. Beauty norms are fundamentally ethnocentric in their reverence of the slender, blue-eyed, blond-haired, fairy princesses of our collective imagination; those marked by disability, age, ethnicity or sexuality need not apply. As feminists move towards a more fractured and multifaceted notion of "woman", the female body has come to be understood as a text, capable of being read as a cultural statement about identity (generally), as well as gender (specifically). The body-as-text is seen as discursively constituted across a number of sites and is in flux, multiple, subject to the whims of fashion, transient and elusive.

This paper serves two main purposes. Firstly, it can be seen that a great deal has been said within feminism about the politics of beauty and the relationship between the constructed self and gender symbolism. This paper functions as a summary of the debate so far and an introduction to the (still current) bones of contention. Secondly, I aim to explore the notion of *becoming* a specific gendered identity, via the construction of an appearance both non-loathsome and discursively significant. The dilemmas women have experienced over their appearance indicate the shift in our understanding of gender from ideological imposition to chosen text, and latterly to an artificial and falsely coherent fiction that our own subversive performances can disrupt. I will begin by reviewing feminist attempts to replace an oppressive and constructed femininity with a more liberating and autonomous feminist aesthetic. I will then suggest that the replication of dualistic readings of image (feminine versus feminist) generated a sense of failure for women who felt that their symbolism of both was inadequate. While the opening up of this space *between* coherent signifiers is fundamental to the feminist attempt to disrupt and destabilise the binary matrix, I will argue that feminists, in their fetishization of signification, have unreasonably demanded that subversion is made textually apparent and that this can somehow represent, subvert or parody that which is promoted as the "real". In this paper, I will suggest that the assumption of the transparent readability and immediate significance of the image is fundamentally flawed; as bodies materialise in our moment by moment interaction, they are fluid while *also* being at the same time constrained by spatial limits on the readability of excess. Furthermore, the belief that we, as cultural theorists, sociologists, feminists or social sophisticates, can make sense of the symbolic body replicates the hierarchical ordering of readable signifiers (and readers) from which we previously wished to escape.

*Femininity as Oppressive*

Within first and second wave feminism, female appearance and the nature of gendered style polarities have been fundamental topics of exploration. Since the initial campaigns for hair and dress reform, in an era when the norms of femininity were first described as constraining and ultimately debilitating, feminists have focused on the ways in which female bodies are given or achieve a gendered identity. Initially, the locus of attention was on disclosing and deconstructing the oppressive and often painful beauty practices with which women seeking social acceptability were expected to comply. Those who failed to achieve beauty, because of their age, shape, ethnicity, disability or sexuality, were not only designated as "other", assessed in terms of standards they were unable to meet, but were expected to make an *effort* ("A" is for attitude) to minimize their unpleasing appearance. In this way, it was argued, female appearance became a fundamental aspect of the subordination of women *as women*, as well as creating a divisive false consciousness among women who believed that they could gain control of their lives by the self-conscious regulation and re-invention of their unruly bodies.

This complex and multifaceted understanding of gendered beauty norms as social constructs, divorced from the pre-determined body and fundamentally artificial and debilitating, was pre-figured by the work of first wave feminists (see Stevenson, 1999). In Charlotte Perkins Gilman's feminist Utopia *Herland*, for instance, which was first published in 1915, the central male character is led to conclude that " ... those 'feminine charms' we are so fond of are not feminine at all, but mere reflected masculinity - developed to please us because they had to please us, and in no way essential to [their] real fulfilment ... " (1979, p. 59). Largely through fiction and satire, Gilman championed a more "natural" and functional mode of dress as of fundamental importance for gaining women's bodily freedom from the constraints of an imposed femininity. This separation of a culturally produced feminine gender from the realm of the biological became a guiding principle of feminist analysis with the publication of

Simone de Beauvoir's *The Second Sex* (1949) and her much quoted assertion that "One is not born, one becomes a woman". Beauvoir, in a comment strikingly similar to Gilman's, suggests that women are required to gain the economic support of men through their production of themselves as erotic objects of display.

> The purpose of the fashions to which she is enslaved is not to reveal her as an independent individual, but rather to offer her as prey to male desires; thus society is not seeking to further her projects but to thwart them. (1988, p. 543)

Here, the saliency of a distinction between sex and gender is achieved within a context of binaries that largely understand the meaning of something by placing it in a relation with its constructed opposite - particularly, in the instance of sex and gender, the opposition between nature and culture, body and mind. Within this context, "sex" is located in the "natural" body, while "gender" is seen as the cultural construction of the historically specific subject in process of becoming. Thus, "gender" for feminists dislocated identity from biological fate, enabling women to contest the naturalisation of sexual difference and insist that the fictive "woman" was constituted within relations of domination and subordination. Initially, then, feminists used the concept of gender to disrupt productively the assumptions of biological foundationalism. "Gender", as created within such an epistemological binary framework, enabled feminists to appropriate the sex/gender distinction to argue for the dominance of the constructed culture-gender in a multiplicity of locales, as well as to deconstruct its naturalised appearance. Increasingly, feminine beauty was exposed as a masquerade, a fiction demanded by the impositions of gendered stereotypes and naturalised by the concealment of its production.

> ... she is not a woman. Her glossy lips and matt complexion, her unfocused eyes and flawless fingers, her extraordinary hair all floating and shining, curling and gleaming, [reveals] the inhuman triumph of cosmetics, lighting, focusing and printing, cropping and composition. (Greer, 1970, p. 60)

Hence, the achievement of a sexed identity was exposed as hard work, not "natural" at all, but indicative of the fictive nature of the supposed unity of the empirical and the symbolic (Braidotti, 1994). The deconstruction of femininity disclosed the extent of women's depreciation within a dualist culture, in which men were able to achieve un-gendered, universal subjectivity and women were always marked as gendered and situated others. Patriarchal norms were therefore exposed as fundamentally *reductive* (gender as expressive of the body) and the feminist aim of liberation by the transcendence of gender (as expressive of cultural norms) was established.

## *Transcending Gender*

Second wave feminists embarked upon a critical and creative reinterpretation of ascribed femininity and a re-evaluation of women's strengths, derived from their position as a site of otherness. Women, it was argued, could achieve full "humanity" by demanding entitlements that had previously been men's by virtue of their sex alone and by rejecting the imposition of an ultimately debilitating femininity, designed for male pleasure and consumption. Such a rejection of naturalism and the constraints of the body was immensely empowering to early second wave feminists.

Anatomy was no longer to be destiny; female potential was not to be limited by the ability to bear and nurture children; the tyranny of a beauty myth that idealised a pre-pubescent smooth-bodied girl as a prototype for feminine desirability was exposed. This apparent primacy of culture became infused with exciting possibilities for those of us who believed that the provision of a feminist counter-culture would lead to a de-differentiated, gender-harmonious future, in which our daughters would fix their cars rather than their hair. Thus, the role of feminists was to be the style champions of a new era: to disrupt convention by dressing for their own pleasure, to celebrate the stretch marks that were the result of bringing forth new life and to reject the oppressive and cumbersome burden of normative femininity (see Davis, 1995). And, for a while, it did appear as if a feminist aesthetic was in process. Women increasingly rejected the discomfort of the corset and the time-consuming bother involved in producing and reproducing the heavily made-up faces and roller set hairstyles fashionable in the 1960s. Like Germaine Greer, they were "sick of the masquerade":

> I'm sick of peering at the world through false eyelashes, so everything I see is mixed with a shadow of bought hairs; I'm sick of weighting my head with a dead mane, unable to move my neck freely, terrified of rain, of wind, of dancing too vigorously in case I sweat into my laquered curls. (Greer, 1970, p. 61)

Women committed to feminism began to discover self-consciously the "reality" of adult women's bodies, opting for comfort and simplicity in their style choices and rejecting the fakery of the demands of femininity. Synnott suggests that, in terms of hair, the new feminist aesthetic involved: " ... medium to short hair lengths, easy to manage, without expensive styles and sets; no wigs, false eyelashes or curlers; no make-up; and axillary and leg hair not only unshaven, but even proudly displayed" (1993, pp. 120-1) - a look which clearly articulates the "natural" as superior to the artificial. A correspondent to *The Guardian* wrote:

> The strength of the feminist movement lies in the fact that they do not need to rely on ... superficiality.... They are fighting the oppression of society - a fight they will never win if they feel obliged to conform to the fashions that society imposes on them. (cited in Wilson, 1985, p. 236)

In a similar way, the assertion that "Black is beautiful" highlighted the racialised as well as sexualised content of (artificial) attractiveness and sought the "natural". Black women increasingly argued that " ... we are being fed an alien concept of beauty which does not reflect our natural image"(Phillips, 1994, p. 57; cf. Mercer, 1987). They pointed out that without the Black Other - " ... women with classical African features of dark skin, broad noses, full lips, and kinky hair" (Collins, 1990, p. 2) - the equation of white-skinned Westerners with beauty would not be possible. The emphasis, then, on the *cultural* construction of sexed, raced and classed identities was productive, in that it allowed those in the civil rights and Black power movements, the radical left and feminists to argue against the view that some were "naturally" inferior or "naturally" less attractive. Certainly, characteristics that were perceived of as biologically fixed at birth would be a lot less amenable to change than a set of socially learnt attitudes and practices. Learnt roles could be unlearnt and one's higher consciousness could be signified by a radical aesthetic that clearly rejected convention. In this way, the "natural" Afro became a symbol of political consciousness that marked the commitment to the cause of Malcolm X and Angela Davis as surely as the diluted butch-dyke look of the 1980s screamed "feminist" to all and sundry.

If, however, alternative beauty ideals *did* prevail, they were short-lived. The Afro was a less enduring style option than Michael Jackson's curly-perm or Naomi Campbell's weave. Jobs still have to be got and kept and those in the labour market continue to face harassment and the threat of dismissal if their appearance is deemed to be "inappropriate". This dilemma has been particularly difficult for Black women to negotiate successfully (see Mama, 1995; Jones, 1995). Lesbians, if we believe the hype, have become "lipsticked" as a rejection of the imposed identities of the diesel-dyke past. It is certain that fashion can no longer be characterised as something that only heterosexual women are forced to participate in - the fashion-spreads in *Diva* now offer an eroticised lesbian visual pleasure under headings such as "Naughty but Nice" (see Chapkis, 1994; Lewis, 1997). And heterosexual women have always been aware of a fundamental conflict between their desire for simplicity and the standards by which they were judged; as Janet Radcliffe Richards pointed out, " ... if women want men, they must be willing to be pleasing to them" (1980, p. 187). After all, she pragmatically concludes, " ... there is nothing to be said for being deliberately unattractive" (1980, p. 193). Feminist writers were all too aware of these dilemmas. Chapkis (1986, pp. 1-3), for example, describes the ridicule she is subjected to because of her visible facial hair. Despite the fact that for years she displayed her " ... hairy underarms and legs with defiant pride", facial hair is still " ...unusual and hence 'unnatural' for a woman. And ugly: *God help me, I too think it ugly* [italics added]" (1986, p. 2). When Chapkis eventually surrenders to social pressure and has electrolysis, guilt haunts her: '"I have failed on both counts", she says, as a woman, as a feminist.

Thus, while many women were concerned to disrupt the conventional standards of beauty and, indeed, have done so to some extent, many remain at odds with their looks - fearing that they will be perceived not only as other, but as "error". In our desire to be inconspicuous, to fit, there is also the hope of security and acceptance. Those areas in which we differ from the norm are only experienced as individualistically original if they have been consciously chosen *and* fit with the expectations of our real and imagined communities (see Haug et. al., 1987). Chapkis is proud of her hairy legs, for they function as a badge of feminist commitment, a chosen identity; her moustache, however, presents an image with which she is uncomfortable, subjectively experienced as symbolising her as "drab, ugly [and] loathsome". Here, women describe the dilemmas and the difficulties involved in the attempt to negotiate an identity that is capable of creating coherence out of chaos; of drawing together that which they categorise as incommensurable. Herein lies their disillusion. The reconfiguration of the binary model defines "femininity" and "masculinity" by just such an incommensurability, as subject positions constructed in a process of mutual exclusion. Hence, Synnott is able to suggest that, in their rejection of conventional femininity, un-feminine feminists approach the masculine. A combination of masculine signifiers - short head hair, visible body hair, and so on - means that " ... the feminist look is *opposite* to the feminine look in all zones and modes ... so it approaches the *masculine* look" (1993, p. 120). In a similar way, Mama (1995) and hooks (1994) indicate further dilemmas faced by women. Both point out that men of all colours are influenced by the dominant notions of female beauty and that Black women's participation in hair-straightening and skin bleaching is less about Black women wanting to be "like" White women than wanting to be attractive, or at least acceptable. One woman ("Mona") interviewed by Mama expresses the same kind of unease discussed by Chapkis. She is described as tall, slim and expensively clad; her hair is naturally fine and straight and her features are "European". However, while Chapkis is defensive over her perceived "ugliness", "Mona" is defensive over her attractiveness. Other Black women accuse her of straightening her hair, of wearing the wrong clothes and of signifying collusion rather than consciousness. While "Mona" says " ... rejection from White people I expect", her Black colleagues' dismissal of her as a White-wannabe is clearly painful (pp. 135-141) and undermines rather than affirms both her attractiveness and her racial identification.

Thus, on the one hand, feminism was seen as the antithesis of feminine; on the other hand, participation in conventional beauty rites was perceived as the antithesis of genuine political commitment. To be a "good" political activist or feminist involved the deliberate rejection of conventional femininity and so re-inscribed one as a failed woman. Such a position created divisiveness, in that it allowed some to be perceived as "better" feminists/activists than others because of their responsibility in choosing the signification of commitment over collusion, and created guilt and unhappiness among those who were reluctant to risk their reconfiguration as "loathsome" within mainstream culture. That women should so *desire* to perform in a way that would locate them within the power spectrum as "feminine" led to disillusionment about the possibilities of overcoming an oppressive "beauty myth" and developing an aesthetic outside of the normative fictions of gender. Moreover, the assumption that wearing Doc Marten boots and 'locks or white stilettos and curly-perms signified the political commitments of different female subjects also assumed the transparency of meaning and that the "real" could be represented and read. Kobena Mercer is doubtful about the possibility of discovering or signifying an authentic self. He quotes the poet Christabelle Peters:

> Sister Carol wears locks and wants a Black revolution
>
> She tours with African dancers around the country
>
> Sister Jenny has relaxed hair and wants a Black revolution
>
> She paints scenes of oppression for an art gallery
>
> Sister Sandra has an Afro and wants a Black revolution
>
> She works at a women's collective in Brixton
>
> Sister Angela wears braids and wants a Black revolution
>
> She spreads love and harmony with her reggae song
>
> All my sisters who want a Black revolution don't care
>
> How they wear their hair. And they're all Beautiful.
>
> (Christabelle Peters, "The politics of hair"; cited in Mercer, 1987, p. 54)

The belief that we could cognitively cast aside our portrayal of gendered femininity and adopt an alternative (significant) subjectivity paid too little attention to cultural constraints, as well as assuming that images are reflective of specific ideologies that are immediately meaningful and readable, irrespective of context. Such a perspective not only takes it for granted that an authentic core of being exists beyond socialisation, but that one can transcend the acculturated body by stepping beyond the boundaries of deception that limit uneducated others. The replication of a binary matrix, defining women as "feminine" *or* "feminist", allows insufficient space for the gaps *between* masculinity and femininity, as well as relegating the majority of women to the position of "cultural dope" (Davis, 1995), a constructed *product* of the binary system, and relinquishing them to the "masquerade" - the very mechanisms which enslave them - in order to avoid being read as other/error. More recent feminist scholarship suggests that women, whether feminist or not, were unable simply to step outside of culture and choose authenticity. We cannot so easily shed our concerns over our appearance with more stringent vigilance or, indeed, by discovering " ... that autonomous feminist subject lurking underneath or outside the constraints of culture" (Davis, 1995, p. 55).

While feminist analyses of gender developed in very different ways, many initially shared the view that the body, as largely "given", pre-figured the inscription of gender; that is, if we believed a body to be biologically female, we enabled the production of an appropriately gendered subject. Thus, the distinction between sex and gender reinforced the view that there exist two fundamentally different kinds of body. So, although feminist work did show that gender, as a cultural phenomenon, is not only capable of polarising the sexes and according value to behaviour that is valueless outside of the gendered interpretive lens, but is also capable of enshrining gendered relations as part of the "natural order", it tended to obscure awareness of other hierarchical ordering systems with which gender interacts. This "fictive" woman, as a product of dualism, is, as Butler (1990) suggests, both exclusionary and normative: the former in that the multiplicity of positions which constitute the subject are ignored; the latter because the replication of binaries enforces heterosexuality. Heterosexuality is a requirement of gender as it is currently constructed, for a "feminine" appearance is that which might be expected to appeal to men; that is, a major meaning of "woman" is sexual attraction to men and availability for them (see also Grant, 1993). The dichotomised thought of modernist philosophies too easily enable the reduction of complex oppressions into binaries; and earlier feminist work failed to follow through the metonymic link between women and other others who are " ... idealizing and appropriating the 'elsewhere' as the feminine" (Butler, 1993, p. 49) and *adding in* other oppressions where appropriate. Thus, a Black drag artist in the Jennie Livingston film *Paris is Burning* (1990) was able to say that, after his operation, he would like to look like " ... a spoiled, rich, White girl"; that is, the " ... archetype of the feminine" (Grant, 1993, p. 177).

However, it is the lack of coherence that exists in the spaces *between* the polarised genders (and sexualities) that was indicated by the "style transgressions" of women in the 1980s that feminists now attempt to colonise. So, despite the pessimism about the possibility of uncovering either an autonomous female subject or an authentic feminist aesthetic, feminist work in the 1970s and 1980s to some extent prefigured the post-structuralist emphasis on the body as text by their insistence on the significance of the readable image and the relevance of appearance. Although we knew that appearance could be read as indicative of character and ideology, our early optimism lay in believing that the deconstruction of oppressive forms of femininity would lay bare this artificiality, to the extent that it would no longer prevail. However, "woman" (even as a fictive category) continues to be more vulnerable to socio-cultural definitions of desirability than does "man" - a reflection of our longstanding placement as relatively subordinate within the enduring binary matrix.

*Enter the Instrumental Feminist Agent: from Masquerade to Mimesis*

The growing awareness that "beauty" functions, not only as a regulatory system and as a mechanism of exclusion, but is capable of articulating hierarchies beyond gender, has led to a more postmodern approach to the production of the female body. The body continues to be perceived as a site of inscription, but a site at which women are the agents *of* inscription, negotiating, rather than ideologically hailed by, the politics of appearance (Smith, 1990). Here it is argued that the body functions as a self-produced object that can be read as a text, the displayed signs by which we perceive the character and status of another. Like any other manufactured object, the body can display a plethora of signs to signify wealth, status, power, capacities, ideology and identity - as well as gender. Femininity becomes, in such an analysis, something that women actively negotiate and "do". While women may well be critical of aspects of idealized femininity - notably weight, with the advent of super-waifs such as Kate Moss - they are embedded within cultural beauty systems and cannot help but collude with them (Bordo, 1993). Bodies become, in Bordo's terms, political battlefields and many of us, even as we are busy deconstructing all that oppressive ideology flooding the media, will also (just to be on the safe side) be buying all the latest miracle creams as well.

It seems, then, that we have witnessed a paradigmatic shift within the last couple of decades, from the body conceptualised primarily as a fixed physiological reality to a perception of the body as a plural and culturally mediated fiction. Feminist work has been important in shifting our focus from the category of the "natural" to that of the "cultural". These are sites with varying degrees of regulatory power that organise and invade our experiences of embodiment. Here, then, feminists and sociologists have, in a real sense, gone beyond nature to re-define both sex *and* gender as artifice, performative and in process. In this way, female biography becomes a reflexive project in which choices over appearance, consumption and life-style are indicative of an identity that is in flux, unfixed and open to a self-conscious re-formulation. If women relate to their bodies as ontologically separable, an objective project to be overhauled with hard work and the right attitude (Giddens, 1991, pp. 75-100), agency is essential. *Without* agency, textual injunctions for self-improvement would be meaningless, in that they would fail to motivate us to participate in the transformation of a self that is perceived (via the textual idealisation of others) as relatively unsatisfactory. This process of individualisation has enabled the proliferation of styles that cross-cut or destabilise fixed status groups, and allows for the development, in the gaps that are created, of the "imagined communities" to which we wish to appeal.

Thus, the value accorded to a *performance* of gender invokes a spectrum of power that is significant only within a *specific interpretive context*; that is, gender is a facet of a complex, and often contradictory, identity. In this way, neither "woman" nor her beauty practices can be seen as object(ive)s straightforwardly determined by the variables of sex and gender, for both are constructed across a multiplicity of sites. Within any given cultural and historical period, attractiveness is textually located in a number of discourses (see Sawchuck, 1988, p. 65). Beauty ideals - the shape of breasts, body, legs - are variable over time, between cultures and *texts*; the Page 3 girl is, for example, typically fuller-figured than the supermodel, and the supermodel is bigger than the new waifs. We can see attractiveness located in "classic" discourses (Chanel, *Vogue*, Princess Diana), as well as a range of "alternatives" (Calvin Klein's "be", *Sky*, Courtney Love). Health discourses intersect with the acceptability of practices such as smoking, drinking, tanning or dieting. Seasonal and spatial variations influence the styles one can be seen in; in the John Waters film *Serial Mom* (1994), for example, one woman kills another for the crime of wearing white pumps after Labour Day. Morality may be signified by the prioritising of "sober" styles, influenced by nationality - the veil, the sari - and, of course, sexuality. The increasing possibilities for "cyborgs" to be created for the manipulation of bodies via surgery or hormonal implants, the awareness of the fragility of bodily boundaries and the need to guard and protect them, all give a new slant to Beauvoir's claim that " ... one is not born a woman". Bodies themselves become a product of culture on the one hand and an individualised project on the other; a text of our own inscribing, ontologically separated from ourselves as object, and, largely, a matter of choice. This emphasis on agency and choice led many feminists to be critical of a perceived "alternative" style imposition and to stress an ideology of individualism.

> Recently I have been the target of a lot of criticism from women ... because they do not like the way I dress and do my hair. They tell me ... that it is not feminist and that I am allowing myself to be exploited by the fashion market ...
>
> Is a woman any less emancipated because she "chooses" to wear make-up and stilettos? ...
>
> Is not the whole point of feminism to help women to realise her right to control her own life and make decisions for herself?
>
> (cited in Wilson, 1985, p. 236).

If the female body can be seen to be constituted across a range of sites, then the reading of beauty practices as the social inscription and repression of the natural body is called into question. If the body can signify a number of fluid subjectivities, our attempt to interpret them can no longer be hailed as a rational decoding, but has to be seen as tentative. Thus, the disruption of the binary matrix, which defined femininity in terms of what it was not, became of primary importance to those with a commitment to feminism. And, in this context, I think that Butler (1990) is spot on to insist upon the drag-like nature of a gendered performance. In drawing our attention to the artificial and constructed nature of appearance, feminists destabilised the meanings of previously fetished items of clothing in their re-appropriation and use of them (Sawchuck, 1988). Chapkis, for example, describes the fun she had with her "Sexual Politics" students.

> I dressed in my very best dyke drag for each lecture, complete with leather and rhinestones ... an attempt to perform gay culture as well as to teach it. My appearance was intended to serve as a model of the pleasures of gender transgression (bright red lipstick under a full blonde moustache) and of a shameless lesbian presence. (1994, p. 14)

The photographer/performer Del(la) Grace (1997) continues to act out and portray the instability of reductive gender categories. She currently dresses as a drag king: butch, but with breasts; a testosterone induced beard, but still soft voiced. The instability of meaning here makes the body/fashion/appearance reflective of *nothing*, rather than of oppressive social hierarchies; that is, a free-floating "image", rather than the "real". Butler insightfully points to the existence of an active feminist agent, who is capable of consciously playing around with the rules of gender. Consider, for example, the women (feminists and lesbians) in the 1980s who resisted easy categorisation by their appropriation of the style spaces between the normative poles. Women who adopted biker jackets and male work boots, but wore them with fancy frocks and fluffy hair, made such an impact that the style filtered down to the mainstream. The playfulness of image construction has the potential to destabilise the fixity of meaning. For Butler, gender becomes the means by which the body is constituted as pre-cultural, constituting " ... the very subject it is said to express". Gender thus becomes a performative re-inscription of the body that is seen, by Butler, as a regulatory fiction that consolidates and is consolidated by heterosexual relations and the assumption of the (binary) correlation between sex and gender. Butler argues that identities have become fluid and performative (although not necessarily voluntaristic - as she is often read). They are no longer required to correspond with the "right" body, nor are they restricted by it. There is no reason as such to prohibit "femininity" being signified by a male body - indeed a man has (fairly recently) won a "women's" beauty contest as a result of his more sophisticated portrayal of the "femininity" being judged than the contest's female participants (Diprose, 1994). The performative subject-in-process thus has the capacity to undermine gender itself; to create both "gender trouble" and de-naturalise the categories of gender and nature. Through subversive bodily acts such as drag, the conventional gender codes are disrupted and subverted; revealed as mimesis, as an imitative structure. If identity is achieved through repeated performances of a fictive self, gender/identity/sexuality cannot be read as revealing an authentic self, but is an effect " ... instituted and inscribed upon the surface of bodies". We must, as Sawchuck points out, move beyond the idea that the "meaning" of the body is either expressive or symbolic of the real. That is, "One cannot assume that a crucifix worn by Madonna is an expression of her essentially Christian nature, or that the wearing of high heels reflects a woman's identification with a patriarchal sexual economy (1988, p. 67).

*Neither*, however, can we assume that the parodic hyperbolization of bodies has the power to destabilise convention straightforwardly or is textually significant outside limited parameters. That is, the practise of inversion as subversion is not easy, straightforward or automatic. Last December, for example, I spent most of my Christmas holiday in a drag club in Cyprus. For the show's grand finale, "Rosie" and "Kitty" spectacularly deconstructed themselves on stage, removing wigs, corsets, padding and make-up to the lyrics "I am what I am and what I am needs no explaining". While this was disconcerting to the men who, previously, had been fondling bodies interpreted, for the occasion, as female, my work into HIV/Aids awareness and my knowledge of the song's significance within that context led me to make meanings from this act that may have been different from those of other members of the audience; meanings that may, in fact, have been different from those intended by the artists themselves. What I am saying is that, if bodies literally "materialise in social interaction" (Haraway, 1990), our meaning-making systems are so complex (and unstable) that the possibilities of a cognitive subversion by inversion are also more complex than has been allowed.

The performance of "subversive" identities is limited by spatial and cultural constraints and the potential readings that may be allowed or disallowed. Many (heterosexualised) spaces reject or disallow identities that are meant to conflict with or subvert dominant readings. No matter how perfect the creation of lipsticked lesbian loveliness was, I doubt if the regulars in my local would read it as subversion, but rather as an illustration of gender tied to the replication of heterosexuality. One is, or one is not, and no space for irony is as yet allowed. Here we must be wary of replicating the view that a position of privilege exists from which those of us "in the know" can snigger at the less far-seeing. Bell, Binnie, Cream & Valentine, for example, argue that "the sexual landscape is ... changing", but "only some of us know it" (1994, p. 37), prioritising "knowledgeable" readings over those of less sophisticated others and assuming that meaning lies primarily in the intentions of individual actors. That the interactive materialisation of subversive bodies is limited spatially and culturally by the range of meanings allowed suggests that insufficient attention has been paid to the ways in which we "read" bodies. Earlier feminist analyses tended to assume that some portrayals of self were "better" or more subversive than others; now, this is re-articulated in the belief that some of us are capable of irony and of its interpretation, whereas others are hopelessly outdated and still take it for real. The prioritisation of authorial intent in the notion of identities as performative thus pays too little attention to: firstly, the complex and contradictory meanings that may be made; and secondly, the impact these meanings have on the reading subject. Bell et al. describe, for example, the growth of a gay "style-skin" look that parodies the skinheads of the 1960s. Style-skins signify a more "dangerous" kind of sexual practice to their peers by their adoption of the hard-boy boots and swastikas of an earlier generation. In rejecting the distinction between the "real" and the "copy", Bell et al. locate transgressive or subversive behaviour in the *intentions* of the author/performer, assuming that, if one is "in the know", one can "see" that such identities are parodies. Certain performances are perceived as chosen, in that other options are consciously rejected. However, in emphasising this conscious production of chosen identities as potentially destabilizing and parodic (of the supposedly real), we pay far too little attention to the reading and reception of these identities by others. Certainly, it is going to be more difficult for Blacks (whether heterosexual or gay) to read the adoption of skinhead style by White gay men "accurately" as parody. If "style-skins" are destabilizing "the uniform of the oppressor", this is hardly likely to reassure Blacks confronted with an image associated, for the majority, with violence against them and hard-line fascism. Such "transgressions" or "subversions" are fundamentally contradictory and point, not only to the importance of reception, but also to the complex nature of relations of domination and subordination.

*Conclusion: One is born ...*

Despite feminist deconstruction, appearances continue to matter a great deal. The success of fitness studios, diet plans, cosmetic surgeons, fashion houses and hair and beauty salons indicates the weight our culture continues to place on physical presentation and the current value of youth and beauty. While the interpretation of bodily signs is culturally contingent and subject to prevailing customs, the stigma attached to those who fail to conform to the beauty myth, whether through a perceived lack of control over their "unruly" appetites or by their age, colour or "deformity", is such that they are not only discriminated against (Wolf, 1990), distanced (sometimes physically as well as socially) from mainstream society, but may also be attributed with negatively valued characteristics (Finkelstein, 1991). Those whose faces fit run the risk of signifying collusion within politically critical communities.

Here I have argued that, in opposition to the earlier understanding of "masquerade" as an imposed role, later feminist theory has stressed "mimesis" as a corrective concept. Mimicry implies a consciousness that masquerade denies; a consciousness that has the potential to resist and subvert accepted or naturalised representations by its deliberate and ironic playfulness. However, while earlier feminist work on beauty has been criticised for encoding an identity in the body and of perceiving the body as an identity, the postmodern emphasis on the body as a collection of signs returns us to the *surface*. For while, in this perspective, images do not represent a pre-existing reality, images and simulacra are themselves taken as constitutive of what is believed to be real. So, rather like the fundamentally cognitive nature of Giddens's subject-as-project, Butler's subject-as-performance assumes a consciousness of alternative subjectivities. As conscious agents of change, it is self-aware artifice, parody and irony that destabilise convention and coherence. It is indeed ironic that, despite the increasing emphasis on the body as a manufactured object, influenced significantly by its historic and spatial locale and its immersion in consumer culture, we remain obsessed with its textual significance and the possibility of reading, if not the "real", at least *something* from it. The problem is that, via these technologies of the self, we are too often believed to be capable of creating a look that is representative *of* self - as if meaning were straightforwardly apparent and instantly readable. However, to suggest that self-aestheticization is reducible to an objectifying process of re-inscribing the female body as textually significant - whether externally imposed *or* part of an internal fantasy of control - is not, in itself, adequate and assumes that identity/beauty occurs on, or is signified by, the external alone.

The emphasis on the surface of bodies was apparent in earlier feminist work, which, in exposing the imposition of an active culture upon a passive nature, thereby investing the "natural body" with its parameters and meanings, replaced the "physical" by the cultural meanings that it "became". The attempt to discover the unconstructed "natural" became lost, however, in a debate over what or who was doing the constructing in the first place. Accounts which derived from Beauvoir paid little attention to women's agency, for gender, as an over-determined construct, was imposed upon its unsuspecting subjects. Later feminists presupposed, in the rejection of determinism and the valorization of a feminist agent who controlled and destabilised the impositions of identity, an instrumental and self-constructed subject. Yet, in the denial of sameness and the prioritising of difference, the specifically female body de-materialises in its oscillation from one identity to another. The subject is replaced by the body and the body is replaced by the text.

> I, and others, started out wanting a strong tool for deconstructing the truth claims of hostile science by showing the radical historical specificity, and so contestability, of *every* layer of the onion of scientific and technological constructions, and we end up with a kind of epistemological electro-shock therapy, which far from ushering us into the high stakes tables of the game of contesting public truths, lays us out on the table with self-induced multiple personality disorder. ... We unmasked the doctrines of objectivity because they threatened our budding sense of collective historical subjectivity and agency and our "embodied" accounts of the truth, and we ended up with one more excuse for not learning any post-Newtonian physics and one more reason to drop the old feminist self-help practices of repairing our own cars. They're just texts anyway, so let the boys have them back.
>
> (Haraway, 1990, p. 186)

I have argued that feminists, in their fetishization of signification, have unreasonably demanded that subversion is made textually apparent and that this can somehow represent, subvert or parody that which is promoted as the "real". However, the assumption of the transparent readability and significance of the image is fundamentally flawed. Firstly, if bodies materialise in social interaction, mimicry's subversion of dominant codes is partial, in that meaning is fluid and cannot possibly be controlled. Secondly, the parodic hyperbolization of roles depends upon the spatial and cultural limits on the readability of excess. Finally, the position of privilege from which we earlier assumed the imposition of the masquerade as a non-ironic assumption of an oppressive role (false consciousness) is in fact replicated in the belief that only some of us are playing and only some of us can see it. But the body is situated materially and politically as well as textually and the empirical evidence available on the meanings made of bodies (anorexic bodies, for example, or those that are HIV positive) suggests that these meanings are not as "in flux" or non-coherent as the postmodern repudiation of signification seems to imply (Probyn, 1988; Haraway, 1990). One *is* born into a position marked by race, ethnicity and sex and influenced by spatial locale, history and wealth, and this limits one's possible becomings. Thus, while the destabilisation of the impositional readings of more powerful others remains of fundamental importance, we cannot alter "gender" or "identity" with a new performative statement. The construction of an identity is a *process* that materialises in social interaction; an interaction that may destabilise identities/meanings in the very production of them, but which can never be guaranteed. While gender is no longer seen as a coherent imposition, we have all too often gone to the opposite analytical extreme, assuming that gender is now merely one other thing to belong to, a matter of cognitive choice or an off-the-peg identity selected from our discursive wardrobe.

*References*

Bartky, S. L. (1990). *Femininity and domination: Studies in the phenomenology of oppression.* London: Routledge, Chapman & Hall.

Beauvoir, S. de. (1988). *The second sex* (H. M. Parshley, Trans.). London: Pan Books. (Original work published 1949).

Bell, D., Binnie, J., Cream, J., & Valentine, G. (1994). All hyped up and no place to go. *Gender, Place and Culture: A Journal of Feminist Geography, 1* (1), 31-47.

Bordo, S. (1993). *Unbearable weight: Feminism, Western culture, and the body.* Berkeley: University of California Press.

Braidotti, R. (1994). *Nomadic subjects: Embodiment and sexual difference in contemporary feminist theory.* New York: Columbia University Press.

Brownmiller, S. (1984). *Femininity.* New York: Simon & Schuster.

Butler, J. (1990). *Gender trouble: feminism and the subversion of identity.* New York: Routledge.

Butler, J. (1993). *Bodies that matter: On the discursive limits of "sex".* New York: Routledge.

Chapkis, W. (1986). *Beauty secrets: Women and the politics of appearance.* Boston, MA: South End Press.

Chapkis, W. (1994) Explicit instruction: Talking sex in the classroom. In L. Garner (Ed.), *Tilting the tower: Lesbians, teaching, queer subjects* (pp. 11-15). New York: Routledge.

Collins, P. H. (1990). *Black feminist thought: Knowledge, consciousness, and the politics of empowerment.* Boston, MA: Unwin Hyman.

Davis, K. (1995). *Reshaping the female body: The dilemma of cosmetic surgery.* New York: Routledge.

Dinnerstein, M., & Weitz, R. (1994). Jane Fonda, Barbara Bush and other aging bodies: femininity and the limits of resistance. *Feminist Issues, 14* (2), 3-24.

Diprose, R. (1994). *The bodies of women: Ethics, embodiment, and sexual difference.* London: Routledge.

Finkelstein, J. (1991). *The fashioned self.* Cambridge: Polity Press.

Giddens, A. (1991). *Modernity and self-identity: Self and society in the late modern age.* Cambridge: Polity Press.

Gilman, C. P. (1979). *Herland.* London: Women's Press. (Original work published 1915).

Grace, D. (1997, July). Photographs, Performance and Presentation given at the Transformations Conference, University of Lancaster.

Grant, J. (1993). *Fundamental feminism: Contesting the core concepts of feminist theory.* New York: Routledge.

Greer, G. (1970). *The female eunuch.* London: MacGibbon & Kee.

Haraway, D. J. (1990). *Simians, cyborgs, and women: The reinvention of nature.* London: Free Association Books.

Haug, F., et al. (1987). *Female sexualization: A collective work of memory* (E. Carter, Trans.). London: Verso.

Henley, N. M. (1977). *Body politics: Power, sex, and nonverbal communication.* Englewood Cliffs, NJ: Prentice Hall.

hooks, b. (1994). *Outlaw culture: Resisting representations.* New York: Routledge.

Jones, L. (1995). *Bulletproof diva: Tales of race, sex and hair.* London: Penguin.

Lakoff, R. T., & Scherr, R. L. (1984). *Face value: The politics of beauty.* Boston, MA: Routledge & Kegan Paul.

Lewis, R. (1997). Looking good: the lesbian gaze and fashion imagery. *Feminist Review, 55,* 92-109.

Livingston, J. (Producer/Director). (1990). *Paris is burning* [Motion picture]. United States: Miramax Films.

Mama, A. (1995). *Beyond the masks: Race, gender, and subjectivity.* London: Routledge.

Mercer, K. (1987). Black hair/style politics. *New formations, 3,* 33-54.

Phillips, M. (1994, Winter). The natural hair page. *Black beauty and hair.*

Probyn, E. (1988). The anorexic body. In A. Kroker & M. Kroker (Eds.), *Body invaders: Panic sex in America* (pp. 201-211). Montreal: New World Perspectives.

Richards, J. R., (1980). *The sceptical feminist: A philosophical enquiry.* London: Routledge & Kegan Paul.

Sawchuck, K. (1988). A tale of inscription/fashion statements. In A. Kroker & M. Kroker (Eds.), *Body invaders: Panic sex in America* (pp. 61-77). Montreal: New World Perspectives.

Smith, D. E. (1990). *Texts, facts, and femininity: Exploring the relations of ruling.* London: Routledge.

Stevenson, K. (1999). Hair today, shorn tomorrow?: Hair symbolism, gender and the agency of self. In J. Rudd & V. Gough (Eds.). *Charlotte Perkins Gilman: Optimist reformer.* Iowa City: University of Iowa Press.

Synnott, A. (1993). *The body social: Symbolism, self and society.* London: Routledge.

Water, J. (Director), Fiedler, J. (Producer), & Tarlov, M. (Producer). (1994). *Serial mom* {Motion picture]. United States: Polar Entertainment Corporation.

Wilson, E. (1985). *Adorned in dreams: fashion and modernity.* London: Virago.

Wolf, N. (1990). *The beauty myth.* London: Chatto & Windus.

Young, I. M. (1990). *Throwing like a girl and other essays in feminist philosophy.* Bloomington: Indiana University Press.

# 6

## "CUTTING UP": MAKING SENSE OF SELF-HARM

### Mairead Owen

> Sitting in private, with a blade at the ready,
>
> Have I got my story right, I hold the blade steady,
>
> It's got to go in deep, right into my arm,
>
> It doesn't hurt, I see the blood, and now I feel calm.

This is a verse from a poem written by a woman I have called Alice. In this article, I would like to explore issues around the troubling phenomenon of people, particularly women, but also men, who cut themselves. I want to link this to theories of the body and the way social scientists try to integrate the body into their ideas of the self.

I am taking an extreme case, which I hope will illuminate the difficulties and stresses that surround the establishment of a stable identity for everyone. "Extreme case" is a phrase and a practice of research of the sociologist Erving Goffman, who suggests that extreme cases can indicate very clearly issues that are submerged or indistinct within everyday life. They can signpost tendencies. In his account, in *Asylums* (1961), of the fight of people put into mental hospitals to retain their identity while the institution systematically seems to try to strip them of that identity, he argues that the same process goes on, more subtly, in less total institutions; for example, big companies, the Civil Service, local government - and schools, colleges and universities.

I should point out that my research has been with women. As feminists have pointed out, traditionally research has been

## "Cutting Up"

highly androcentric, reading man as the generic subject when in reality the "knowledge" so produced is highly gendered (e.g. Thiele, 1992). There are so many lectures, papers, articles and books in which the generic "man" is discussed and then, at ten to the hour or the penultimate page, there is the brief discussion of the exception - women. So it is with no apology that, in taking this extreme case, women will be put in the foreground, their experiences explored and, where relevant, the applicability of the research to men indicated.

My starting point is a research project that is not a research project. Some years ago, in my work as a counsellor, I had come across a small number of women who cut themselves. It needs to be clarified that these women were not presenting with the problem of cutting and in fact the problems with which they had arrived at the agency were often quite practical, information-giving situations. Others had more emotional problems, but the cutting emerged only indirectly. The practice seemed very worrying and I felt I needed to know more. However, when the literature on incidences of cutting was researched, it seemed that there were, with a few exceptions, broadly two sources of information. One set of research work looked at hospitalised patients and the other set looked at people in prison. The general trend within the conclusions was, not surprisingly, that the people, mostly women, in hospital were psychiatrically disturbed and the practice was part of their illness; the people, again mostly women, in prison were categorised as trouble-making attention seekers. As Caroline Moorhead suggested in *New Society* some years ago, in relation to cutting in Holloway Prison:

> ... the psychiatrists see their actions in terms of a *cri de coeur*, whether from a woman in a state of severe depression, or from a "hysterical

psychopath", one who, theatrically and histrionically, is playing out her own feelings of frustration. (1985, p. 42)

However, I found that the women I had met myself were functioning "normally" in the community and moreover, far from being attention seekers, went to great lengths to conceal what they were doing; for example, by wearing long sleeves and thick stockings in the hottest of weather, to conceal the usual sites of cutting, on the arms and legs.

It is intriguing that recently, when two women approached me, one a mother of a daughter who cut and one who had been a cutter but who has now stopped the practice, they mentioned that, as both the women who cut had got better, they had started to wear shorter skirts. The younger mentioned quite specifically that she thought this was because she wished it to be known that she was cutting and that she wished to be helped. In other words, it was a sign of recovery.

Research often discusses instances of cutting as "para-suicides". It is essential to stress that those I met at the beginning and those who have since spoken to me are adamant that cutting up is not a failed suicide attempt.

> It's hard to explain the feeling you get,
>
> I watch the blood dripping, it's warm and wet,
>
> It's not deep enough, I was too scared,
>
> I don't want to die, I just want to hurt.

As Alice's words indicate, the women in the research have no intention of killing themselves. Ironically, to those outside the practice, they do not have the intention of harming themselves. Alice even told me that she took advantage of any cuts or grazes from "real" accidents to cut those, because " ...

## "Cutting Up"

you don't want to be scarred all over, so you just open the same ones all the time".

Two aspects of this phenomenon, therefore, struck me. Firstly, that the verdict on the women in psychiatric hospitals and the women in prisons did not accord at all with the women to whom I had spoken. Secondly, my meeting with the women in the community seemed so accidental that I wondered if it could be that the practice was much more widespread within and across societies than had been thought.

By definition, I had become interested in something that would be very difficult to research: the hypothesis that many women who were living in the "normal" community were cutting themselves and going to great lengths to ensure that their practice remained secret. Yet I feel it is important that something should be said, so that women and men will be empowered by the knowledge that they are not alone. Moreover, at a theoretical level, it seems to turn commonsense notions about self-preservation and the care of the body upside down.

My research project is, therefore, not at all a conventional one. Over the last few years, I have mentioned the topic in various forums, often in relation to other topics. Women have approached me or given permission to other women to mention their participation in the practice, often in very elliptical ways, so I do not set out to look for my empirical informants, but wait to be approached, respecting the secrecy that women may want to maintain. I think the project could safely be labelled long-term! But I am now beginning to build up a stock of very individual accounts, which nevertheless do seem to have certain themes in common. I must mention that so far no Black women are in the sample and no women over about 45, though one informant told me about an older friend, in her sixties, who cuts.

It does seem from the limited work on this topic that women are more likely to cut themselves than men are. Alix

Kirsta, in her book *Deadlier than the Male* (1994, p. 13), suggests a figure of four to one. Graham Houghton (1998, p. 14) offers a figure of two to three times more women than men. My own experience in listening to women who cut coincides very much with the picture painted by Kirsta and by Houghton. Kirsta describes the ritual of cutting by one of her respondents: the clean bathroom, bandages and antiseptic, the new razor blade, the care not to do too much damage so as not to attract the attention of family, friends or the medical profession, while Houghton explains how "Rachel ... carves patterns on her skin and, when she's finished, stems the blood with toilet paper, then carefully bandages the wounds" (1998, p. 14). Kirsta also describes the effect on the cutter:

> And as the blood begins to flow more freely, the effect begins to work: Zandra is at last released from the angry tension ... the tightness, the unbearable tension, all are suddenly gone. Instead, a sense of peace and of being fully alive replaces the zombie-like numbness. (Kirsta, 1994, p. 310)

Zandra speaks of the tension building over the weeks; the knowledge that she would cut herself again and then the relief, until the next time. Women within the research described exactly the same feeling of a build-up of tension until they had to cut, and then the peace. It is striking that they report no pain. One respondent speculated that this " ... could have something to do with the chemicals in your veins". She believed that the build-up of tension and adrenalin led to a degree of anaesthesia. Alix Kirsta points out how little research has been done into this phenomenon and particularly stresses the fact that it would seem that " ... cutting continues to confound the experts, especially where it occurs among the *normal* [italics added] population" (Kirsta, 1994, p. 311).

## "Cutting Up"

Obviously, the question arises of how prevalent it is ritually to cut one's own body in this way. Houghton (1998, pp. 14) states that: "An estimated 0.75 per cent of the population - one in every 130 people - are active self-injurers", with cutting as the major manifestation of self-injury. However, this seems to be a very difficult phenomenon to estimate. It is true that the women who do this must have problems; however, it seems very possible that those admitting to having such problems are a small minority of those cutting and that there are indeed a chilling number of women - and men - in the community who are doing so. It shocked many, for example, that on the first anniversary of the suicide in 1994 of Kurt Cobain, the rock musician, there was a spate of letters from readers of both sexes to *NME* (the *New Musical Express*) and *Melody Maker*, two music papers, conveying their despair, their empathy for Courtney Love, his wife, and describing how their own feelings led to their cutting themselves. When Richey James of the Manic Street Preachers group talked of his own cutting, also in *NME*, a typical letter said, "I'd never told anyone about cutting myself. ... since I discovered that Richey cuts himself, it gave me feelings of affinity with him. I feel I share my secret with him"; and another said, "He hasn't encouraged me to harm myself, he has just made me feel less alone" (Smith, 1995, p. 2). Again, Roger Tredre and Ruth Fisher (1995, p. 3), in talking about the discussion that had grown up in the musical press, reported similar correspondence. One writer said, "I could burst and then I cut my skin and everything's fine". Elizabeth Wurtzel, in the best seller *Prozac Nation* (1995), described how she would spend lunch times cutting her legs as she listened to her music.

It seems to me that, as feminists, social scientists, philosophers, human beings, we need to understand the relationship between self and body, not just as an intellectual puzzle, but in order to comprehend the situation of women and men for whom that new razor in the bathroom seems to be the only answer to their social and psychological circumstances. While academics may think out concepts of the body/mind relationship as a model, which must attain internal coherence and plausibility, it seems essential that any theory so produced must be able to comprehend the actions and feelings of real people in the everyday world. As Wittgenstein said:

> I then thought what is the use of studying philosophy if all that it does for you is to enable you to talk with some plausibility about some abstruse questions of logic, etc., and if it does not improve your thinking about the important questions of everyday life? (Malcolm, 1966, p. 39)

The relationship of people to their bodies seems highlighted in the practice of cutting. Ostensibly, this practice seems a complete exemplar of the Cartesian principle of duality. Surely the self here is the self experiencing and acting upon a body that is irretrievably a thing, quite estranged from the thinking self, used as an instrument to be punished or utilised in that attention seeking described in the literature. Susan Bordo (1992), in her work on anorexia, has quoted the long history of the body as despised and denigrated.

It seems that, even though social commentators are trying to move away from this denigration, it has become a facet of Western hegemony, everywhere the "common sense" of everyday, so that, as Bordo suggests, within this dualist axis which casts the body as despised, it is experienced as alien, it is confinement and limitation, it is the enemy out of control (Bordo, 1992, p. 94). Many feminist writers (e.g. Gatens, 1991, p. 92; Grosz, 1994, p. 5; Kappeler, 1994, p. 75) have commented on the fact that, while Western thought has worked in dualities: e.g. culture/nature, male/female, public/private, and the paradigm of them all, mind/body, the point is that, as Beauvoir (1949) stressed, it is not solely that the world and the way we think about it is "dualised", but that these dichotomies are not equal. They are not the *yin* and *yang* of Eastern mysticism, complementary and equal. They are superior and inferior, but, even more, they are A and non-A; the term of "the Other" refers to a lack, a state of non-being. It is with the recognition that Cartesian duality in regard to mind and body is not only inadequate, but particularly a gendered concept, in that these terms of alterity are also mapped on to male and female with woman as Beauvoir's eternal "Other", that feminists have been particularly active in attempting to think of the body in new ways. While there has in recent years been a renewed interest in theorising the body, and indeed there have always been oppositional ideas to the duality "common sense", I would claim that feminists have been in the vanguard of this movement, though even they have sometimes lost sight of the material body.

Kathy Davis, in discussing feminist efforts to conceptualise the body and to claim oppositional work to patriarchal, phallocentric theories of the body, points out that:

> While there has been a wealth of feminist scholarship devoted to exploring the particularities of embodiment, recent feminist theory on the body has displayed a marked ambivalence towards the material body and a tendency to privilege the body as metaphor. Priority is given to the deconstructive project - that is, to dismantling the mind/body split in Western philosophy or debunking gendered symbols and dichotomies rather than to attending to individuals' actual

material bodies or their everyday interactions with their bodies and through their bodies with the world around them. (Davis, 1997, p. 15)

Similarly, Helen Marshall states that:

Although I am basically sympathetic to the thrust of argument that we must reconceptualise the body, and find much of the more recent work on how to do so very exciting, I am concerned that so much attention is being paid to nomenclature and theory, and so little to the lived experiences and data .... (Marshall, 1996, p. 253)

It is with some very tentative empirical research that I would like to pursue this enterprise of linking actual material bodies to social science theories. While, as I shall explain, this is rather an unusual study, accidental and limited, I think the point that theories of the body seem, in spite of efforts to break away from the cycle, always to become exceptionally *disembodied* is a most important one. In this article, I would like to suggest that our theories do need to take account of actual bodies and, moreover, that those theories need to see the embodied Subject as an active agent, "speaking the body". Berthelot (1995, p. 15) also makes this point when he suggests that, in the effort to move from a mechanistic model, we have substituted a "signifying interiority", ignoring the organic reality of the body

As feminists have been aware, "By imprisoning 'the Other' in her/his body, privileged groups - notably, white, Western, bourgeois, professional men - are able to take on a god's eye view as disembodied Subjects" (Davis, 1997, p. 10). This "god's eye view" is exceptionally difficult for women to take on. Women do live in the body. The experiences of a female body, of menstruation, of pregnancy, of parturition, of lactation, of menopause, are constant reminders in all their immediacy that we are embodied subjects. The fiction of the "ghost in the machine" is difficult to maintain when one is aware of the constantly changing corporeal self. Not only do women live these experiences, but they also live in a social world structured in the equation of all women, whether subject to them or not, with these experiences. Gatens describes the lived experience of sexed bodily subjectivities (Barrett, 1988, p. xxxiii). Grosz (1994, p. 10) talks of how to " ... bypass the dualisms which dominate traditional thinking, while providing the basis for an understanding of difference (i.e. a non-oppositional notion of difference) that is useful, perhaps necessary to reformulate male and female relations". Braidotti (1991, p. 73) has stressed " ... that there is only one substance, and that it is corporeal. ... [T]here is a common level of immanence of things, a profound unity of being". Perhaps using this as a basis, we can begin to apprehend how a woman experiences her body as she cuts her own skin and her blood flows. In none of the reports is there a hint that the body is felt as the enemy or as the machine that contains the ghost, as the container for the Cartesian subject. "Dig the blade in; as you cut through the skin, you feel better", suggested Alice. She is her body.

It is not only an insistence on the materiality of the body that marks the feminist project, but also a recognition at the same time that the body is not the result of a biological determinism. The body is problematic. While no one would deny the biological inheritance, the infinite plasticity of the human entity, the way in which society constructs and moulds the seemingly given body, must be recognised. In this enterprise it has been the postmodernist, post-structuralist approaches to the body of Lacan, Derrida, Deleuze and, above all, Foucault that have stimulated discussion by feminists.

> Foucault's studies on the regimes of the prison, the asylum and the clinic, as well as the history of sexuality, were seminal in understanding the body as object of processes of discipline and normalization. Through his work, the body came to be seen more generally as a metaphor for critical discussions which link power to knowledge, sexuality and subjectivity. (Davis, 1997, p. 3)

However, this growing interest in the body (Morgan & Scott, 1993) does seem to drift constantly into a theoretical and, paradoxically, structuralist analysis, which potentially loses sight of the experience of people in the day-to-day world. Also, while Foucault (1977) is at pains to insist on the diffuse nature of power and the fact that all take part in the discourses of power, there is nevertheless an almost totalitarian determinism about his pictures of the clinic, the prison and the asylum under the surveillance of the panoptic big brother. While Foucault points out that the watcher is also watched, there is little discussion to suggest that any real power rests with those who are the ultimate objects of the gaze (Fraser, 1989).

In their project to understand gender and sexual difference, it is not surprising that one of the most pervasive and continuing themes for feminists has to be the attempt to theorise the body. It is the female body that is the stigmatizing mark that denotes a member of the "second sex". As we theorise sex/gender, we automatically encounter the body.

Elizabeth Grosz's suggestion of the Mobius strip metaphor has intrigued many other researchers. She suggests that the

## "Cutting Up"

"... Mobius strip, the inverted three-dimensional figure eight ... has the advantage of showing the inflection of mind into body and body into mind, the ways in which, through a kind of twisting or inversion, one side becomes another ... (Grosz, 1994, p. xii).

Judith Butler's suggestion (1990, 1993) that gender is performance implies that the body too is performance, with inside expressing outside and outside in.

Perhaps it is with the French feminists, with their notion of writing the body, that the impressions gained from the women to whom I spoke resonated most. Cixous suggests that, "Locked in the body, the body is all women have to express their madness" (Gatens, 1991, p. 120), which is surely the most condensed representation of women who cut themselves. Cixous suggests that " ... we need to struggle for a social organization and a way of thinking and speaking where both men and women can live the specificity of their bodies and their desires" (Gatens, 1991, p. 121). The French feminists urge that we should enter into language, to write the body. As Cixous observes in her much quoted "The Laugh of the Medusa" (1997, p. 356), "*In body* - more so than men who are coaxed toward social success, toward sublimation, women are body". It seemed to me that those women to whom I spoke were literally writing the body. They were bypassing language and expressing with and through their bodies the things they wanted to voice. Alice showed me one particular scar, which she mentioned frequently and which she said was a cut which she had kept re-opening on its original site, but which she had re-opened in a careless way one day and had not kept quite to the earlier scar, so that it no longer followed the original straight line. "Look, it's like a mouth", she said, and, later in the conversation, "That mouth is there because I missed". The resonances of Freud, of Irigaray, were difficult to resist. Cutting has been compared to anorexia and to bulimia as a means of control, of demonstrating mastery of that alienated body. In the readings and from talking to those who cut, it seemed to me that this did not convince. The body and the mind here seemed one, the body being the expression of all the thoughts, feelings and desires that, with that body, could be termed the self.

It is important in attempting to theorise the body that historical specificities are not overlooked as we struggle to a conceptualisation. Those feminists who stress the differences between women draw attention to the dangers of essentialism and universalism in theorising. "For women to answer the question of the individual subject in materialist terms is first to show, as the lesbians and feminists did, that supposedly 'subjective', 'individual', 'private' problems are in fact social problems, class problems" (Wittig, 1997, p. 226). Ann Rosalind Jones (1997, p. 377) quotes Wittig's words, "It remains. . . for us to define our oppression in materialistic terms, to say that women are a class, which is to say that the category 'woman', as well as 'man', is a political and economic category, not an eternal one". There were no Black women in my small sample. Do Black women express their distress in the same way as the women I met? Terri had cut, but no longer did so. Is the stopping of cutting a function of her own movement through life or is it a function of the different age cohorts? Is age a factor? Such factors as class, income and sexuality also need to be explored. What is the experience of men who cut? "It is clear that the material body is a critical symbolic resource for cultural expression, and although "the body" can be studied as a discursive construction, its symbolic form is *always* constructed in interaction with real material bodies" (Balsamo, 1996, p. 159)

Susan Bordo (1992) has suggested that women can take on "male" power – power as self-mastery - and, paradoxically, feel empowered or liberated by the very bodily norms and practices that constrain or enslave them. It is true that cutting is very obviously self-destructive and is often equated with the

## "Cutting Up"

anorexia or bulimia which is the subject of Susan Bordo's discussion in "Anorexia nervosa: psychopathology as the crystallization of culture". Indeed Alice, who has recovered from cutting and has been for counselling, said that, after having had the counselling, "I came to realise that it was a method of being in control" and certainly it seems to be the understanding of counsellors that cutting, anorexia and bulimia represent this desire for control in an uncontrollable world. "The constant downward trend [of the scale] somehow comforts me, gives me visible proof that I can exert control. [The diet] is the one sector of my life over which I and I alone wield total control" (Bordo, 1992, p. 97). The body in this thinking is seen as the instrument on which to demonstrate the control of the "mind". Interestingly, in those who had not discussed their experience with a counsellor, their comments reflected both that of Zandra in the previously quoted picture from Alix Kirsta (1994) and also Alice's poem. Here, the act of cutting and the ritual surrounding it was the result of a stress that mounted to unbearable heights and that was calmed and relieved by the cutting; not so much control of an alien body, but a speaking of the body.

Agency, acting as a thinking, self-reflexive subject, does not necessarily have to have a positive outcome, though many would argue that autonomy and self-direction have value in themselves, whatever the result of exercising those freedoms. Action can be self-defeating or ill-conceived. By reflecting on their actions and the outcomes, women mount a continuing process of growth and reactive activity. Alice thought that women who cut themselves were usually young, and this certainly mirrored her own experience, though my own suggested a wider range of ages. We forget that the research process is often like a snapshot, in that the people who speak to the researcher become fixed in the resulting publications like butterflies caught on the pin, but of course they are not. The life cycle continues for them. Cutting can be an almost rational response to a situation. If the situation changes, if the oppression changes, then so does the action. As Balsamo suggests, "These arrangements are historical articulations that must be continually reproduced .... But the fact that these arrangements must be continually reproduced also suggests the possibility that these articulations can be disrupted" (1996, p. 162). It seems to me that, if we do not have direct knowledge of a practice like cutting, we automatically assume that the cutters are victims of the system. The practice of cutting seems to the outsider to be self-defeating and I am certainly not recommending it. However, Alice believed that women who cut "often grow out of it" - and the word "grow" had a whole weight of meaning. Jan, one of the first women who spoke to me about this, had a history of terrible abuse, and said quite simply that if she did not continue to cut, she might commit suicide. Women listened to their bodies, to their tensions and stresses, and took the course of action that met their needs of the time and their situation most directly.

It is important, as ever, to pick up on theories of structure and agency here, and understand that work must be done to alleviate the conditions of society that bring people to these actions and to recognise that they are actions; and also that they are a thoughtful response to the cutters' situation. In a very different context, I have recognised the concept of "distance" employed by women in their day-to-day lives (Owen, 1997). In their experience of identity, women can live the experience described by Braidotti (1991) of identity as problematic and changing, but particularly they can be self-aware, aware that their actions, beliefs and feelings can be dissonant. Women constantly play highly defined roles which, within a patriarchal and capitalist society, may at best be not of their choosing and ill-fitting in day-to-day living. At worst, they are lived out in fear of retribution if they do not adhere to the script. Patriarchy does not, of course, mean the rule of men over women, but the rule of a class of powerful men over women, older and younger men, ethnic minorities, those not heterosexual or able-bodied, and children; these groups too do not write the scripts. Berger and Luckmann (1966) were concerned that one of the dangers of modern industrial society, with multiple roles for each individual, was that modern man (*sic*) might come to act out those roles without commitment and identification. Women already, and perhaps for centuries, have lived their imposed roles with distance and detachment, as do other "non-patriarchs"; with a self-awareness, with amusement in some areas of life, with cool self-understanding in others (Owen, 1997). One of my respondents said, "I know it is not going to solve anything, but gradually the tension rises and it's the only thing to do"; and Kirsta (1994, p. 314) quotes a similar response, "I did it because I was screaming inside …. The blood did my crying for me and I didn't have to bother anyone with how I felt". The body is making its demands and the woman recognises that the self has various locations. The body literally incorporates the Subject. The woman inscribes herself in the materiality of her existence. The body bypasses the entry into language and speaks directly. At the same time, she knows that her actions are not productive, that they will not resolve the social problem *and* that many of the problems will be resolved, the rising tension will disappear, there will be a physical relief from the effects of conforming to those roles which may merely constrict her physical and mental integrity or which may threaten it. It is a dangerous research practice to believe that human beings are self-deluding, that they do not know, that their actions, no matter how extraordinary, are not stemming from a thinking Subject. We need a theory that can encompass this. Evelyn Fox Keller, in discussing the work of the scientist Barbara McClintock, has protested against the dichotomies of science and offered a vision:

## Gender in Flux

Instead of aiming toward a cosmic unity of paired opposites - a unity typically excluding or subsuming one of the pair - respect for difference remains content with multiplicity as an end in itself .... McClintock's practice of science offers another possibility: it teaches us about a world in which self and other, mind and nature, survive neither in mutual alienation nor in symbiotic fusion, but in structural integrity. (Keller, 1992, p. 49)

We need that world of "structural integrity" to understand and help the men and women who cut. Here are the last two verses of Alice's poem:

> No cut or gash, will release the pain I feel inside,
>
> But for a time, it helps it to subside,
>
> It helps me live from week to week,
>
> I don't know why I am so weak.
>
>
> The cut heals up, and back comes the pain,
>
> It's time to start over again,
>
> You come to a time, when you realise, what it's all about,
>
> It's the inner pain, that needs cutting, but leave the blade out.

Alice gave me the poem as she was leaving after our interview. I keep wondering whether or not to get in touch about the ambiguity of that last phrase. Is the emphasis on "leave" or on "blade"? Has she decided not to use the blade again, as she recognises that it is not the solution or, in spite of her realisation, does the blade need to be left out - and ready. I have not asked her yet. I am not sure if there is an answer.

*References*

Balsamo, A. (1996). *Technologies of the gendered body: Reading cyborg women.* Durham, NC: Duke University Press.

Barrett, M. (1988). *Women's oppression today: The marxist/feminist encounter.* (Rev. ed.) London: Verso.

Beauvoir, S. de (1988). *The second sex.* (H. M. Parshley, Trans.). London: Pan Books. (Original work published 1949).

Berger, P. L., & Luckmann, T. (1966). *The social construction of reality: A treatise in the sociology of knowledge.* Garden City, NY: Doubleday.

Berthelot, J.-M. (1995). The body as a discursive operator: On the aporias of a sociology of the body. *Body and Society, 1,* 13-25.

Bordo, S. (1992). Anorexia nervosa: Psychopathology as the crystallization of culture. In H. Crowley & S. Himmelweit (Eds.), *Knowing women: Feminism and knowledge* (pp. 90-109). Cambridge: Polity Press.

Braidotti, R. (1991). *Patterns of dissonance: A study of women in contemporary philosophy.* (E. Guild, Trans.). Cambridge: Polity Press.

Butler, J. (1990). *Gender trouble: Feminism and the subversion of identity.* New York: Routledge.

Butler, J. (1993). *Bodies that matter: On the discursive limits of "sex".* New York: Routledge.

Cixous, H. (1997). The laugh of the Medusa (K. Cohen & P. Cohen, Trans.). In R. R. Warhol & D. P. Herndl (Eds.), *Feminisms: An anthology of literary theory and criticism* (pp. 347-362). Basingstoke: Macmillan. (Original work published 1975).

Davis, K. (Ed.) (1997). *Embodied practices: Feminist perspectives on the body.* London: Sage.

Foucault, M. (1977). *Discipline and punish: The birth of the prison* (A. Sheridan, Trans.). London: Allen Lane. (Original work published 1975).

Fraser, N. (1989). *Unruly practices: Power, discourse and gender in contemporary social theory.* Cambridge: Polity Press.

Gatens, M. (1991). *Feminism and philosophy: Perspectives on difference and equality.* Cambridge: Polity Press.

Goffman, E. (1961). *Asylums: Essays on the social situation of mental patients and other inmates.* Garden City, NY: Doubleday.

Grosz, E. (1994). *Volatile bodies: Toward a corporeal feminism.* Bloomington, IN: Indiana University Press.

Houghton, G. (1998, April 14). Scarred by a secret shame. *The Guardian*, p. 14.

Jones, A. R. (1997). Writing the body: Toward an understanding of *l'ecriture feminine*. In R. R. Warhol & D. P. Herndl (Eds.), *Feminisms: An anthology of literary theory and criticism* (pp. 371-383). Basingstoke: Macmillan. (Original work published 1981).

Kappeler, S. (1994/95). From sexual politics to body politics. *Trouble & Strife, 29/30*, pp. 73-79.

Keller, E. F. (1992). How gender matters; or Why it's so hard for us to count past two. In G. Kirkup and L. S. Keller (Eds.), *Inventing women: Science, technology and gender* (pp. 42-56). Cambridge: Polity Press. (Original work published 1983).

Kirsta, A. (1994). *Deadlier than the male: Violence and aggression in women*. London: HarperCollins.

Malcolm, N. (1966). *Ludwig Wittgenstein: A memoir*. (Rev. ed.) London: Oxford University Press.

Marshall, H. (1996). Our bodies ourselves: Why we should add old-fashioned empirical phenomenology to the new theories of the body. *Women's Studies International Forum, 19*, (3), 253-265.

Moorhead, C. (1985, April 11). The strange events at Holloway. *New Society*, pp. 40-42.

Morgan, D. H. J., & Scott, S. (1993). Bodies in a social landscape. In S. Scott & D. H. J. Morgan (Eds.), *Body matters: Essays on the sociology of the body* (pp. 1-21). London: Falmer Press.

Owen, M. (1997). Re-inventing romance: Reading popular romantic fiction. *Women's Studies International Forum, 20*, (4), 537 - 546.

Smith, A. (1995, March 31). Is this music to die for? *The Guardian*, p. 2.

Thiele, B. (1992). Vanishing acts in social and political thought: Tricks of the trade. In L. McDowell & R. Pringle (Eds.), *Defining women: Social institutions and gender divisions* (pp. 26-35). Cambridge: Polity Press. (Original work published 1987).

Tredre, R., & Fisher, R. (1995, March 26). Despair cuts a generation adrift. *The Observer*, p. 3.

Wittig, M. (1997). One is not born a woman. In S. Kemp & J. Squires (Eds.), *Feminisms* (pp. 220-226). Oxford: Oxford University Press.

Wurtzel, E. (1995). *Prozac nation: Young & depressed in America: A memoir.* Boston, MA: Houghton Mifflin.

# 7

# CARING OR NOT CARING: ACADEMIC RESPONSES TO HOUSEHOLD AND LABOUR MARKET CHANGE[1]

## Jane Wheelock

Starting with an overview of the theory and practice of gender disadvantage in the 1970s and 1980s, this chapter aims to spell out what theoretical debate and empirical research about the household have to contribute to the current policy agenda. To some extent, my own academic career has paralleled and foreshadowed some of the features of this period of academic history. I studied Marxist theory as a mature student in the 1970s, while bringing up two young sons. Selma James was calling for wages for housework at the time, but for most of the mothers in the Scottish Women's Movement, from which I got support, this was the last thing that we wanted. After all, Engels (1940/1884) was adamant that it would only be by entering the labour market that women would overcome patriarchy. To think that a New Labour Government, so anxious to distance itself from "Old Labour", should in 1998 introduce a National Childcare Strategy with such thoroughly Marxist credentials! The Childcare Strategy is part of a package for "making work pay" - in this case for mothers.

In the 1970s, the domestic labour debate was raging in the pages of *New Left Review* and *Capital and Class*.[2] It was

---

[1] With thanks to *Capital and Class*, who gave permission to publish this slightly revised version of "'Don't care was made to care': The implications of gendered time for policies towards the household", which appeared in *Capital and Class*, 75, Autumn 2001, pp. 173-184.

[2] Some of the key articles have been reproduced in Himmelweit (2000)..

an almost exclusively theoretical debate on the role of domestic labour (more usually understood as housework) and social reproduction (caring for the young, the old and the sick) under capitalism. It came in the wake of Gary Becker's exegesis of a neo-classical new household economics model (1980/1965), for which Becker drew on the work of Margaret Reid (Yi, 1996). Both Left and Right took it as given that domestic work was done by women - in which they were correct, as later empirical work confirmed.

But how were these philosophers to change the world? Of course, it was important that, for the first time since Engels, Marxists were seriously theorising the position of women. It was the beginning of an academic revolution, in which one discipline after another began to pay attention to sexist bias; but empirical work was going to show that overcoming the reproduction of gendered power relations would be no pushover. The Equal Pay Act, passed in 1970, but not implemented until five years later, is a case in point; women's hourly wages still lag behind men's over a quarter of a century later. The economic and political changes to come were to prove tougher than either the Marxists or the feminists of the 1970s were bargaining for. The agenda for change was seized by the forces of capital, aided and abetted by two decades of political dominance by the New Right. Power-dressed women in sharp suits who employed nannies to look after their children have been, sadly, some of the most notable beneficiaries of a labour market that has become steadily more unequal in the rewards that it pays out (Humphries & Rubery, 1992; Gregson & Lowe, 1993).

It was a sociologist, Ann Oakley (1974), who asked the hitherto undreamed question of what would happen if you analysed housework in the same way as the more familiar form of (men's) labour market work. It was, if you like, an empirical study of the labour process in a household setting. Following Oakley, the gender blindness of previous studies of work was then challenged by all kinds of empirical studies of women in the labour market: as members of co-operatives in rural East Anglia (Wajcman, 1983); as workers in cigarette factories in Bristol (Porter, 1982); as clerical workers (Crompton, Jones & Reid, 1982); and so on. This empirical agenda continued throughout the 1980s and, at every step, the interwoven character of the women's labour market and domestic lives became more and more apparent (e.g. Yeandle, 1984). And, although women might protest that they were working for "extras", these extras, when they were pressed, turned out to be paying the mortgage, ensuring that the family had a holiday or buying the children's clothes (Stubbs & Wheelock, 1990). Households were coming to rely upon more than one wage and women were increasingly shouldering a double burden of (often part-time) labour market work alongside other domestic and caring duties.

So were there any circumstances in which men would be prepared to take on housework and be responsible for the children? It seemed that a certain number of middle class "*Guardian* New Men" could make their employment flexible enough to share bringing up their children with their professionally trained partners - as indeed happened in my own household when my youngest was born. But, for example, in households without wage earners, fathers sometimes did even less than when they had been in work (Morris, 1985; Bell & McKee, 1985). In the mid-1980s, when male unemployment in North East England was at record levels, I got a small grant from the Equal Opportunities Commission to study households in which men, typical of the local "smokestack" labour market, had become unemployed, while their wives continued to be employed. This, it transpired, was a situation in which traditional gender roles did indeed get eroded and it was even possible to find the occasional man doing the ironing or cleaning the windows, with appreciable numbers describing their daily domestic and childcaring routine in considerable detail; but these changes could be very difficult for women as well as men to handle (Wheelock, 1990b).

I became fascinated by the way in which the lives that women and men led in their households were shaped and moulded by the changing ways in which capitalism ordained that they gain their livelihoods. Feminist empirical work of the 1980s meant that women were at last appearing as subjects in their own right in the social sciences and the relationship between patriarchy and capitalism was being theorised (e.g. Cockburn, 1983). Yet a danger was beginning to surface, in that gender was being considered only in terms of women, rather than as a relationship between women and men. Undertaking research at the level of the household can counter that danger (Wheelock & Oughton, 1996). Once the social sciences are informed by feminism, studying the behaviour of people in their households can encompass the presence of gender as a power relationship between women and men, in turn structured by the wider class, economic and social context in which the household is located.

But, in investigating the interface between the individual, the household, the formal economy and social institutions, it becomes clear that the traditional economic simplification of social actors who maximise their individual well-being is called into question by the way that people behave in the real world. Simplified models, nevertheless, have great academic appeal and the economic model of behaviour has been eagerly embraced by political science as the basis for public choice theory (see Dunleavy, 1991) and indeed by some currents in analytical

Marxism (Elster, 1985; Roemer, 1986). Whether implicitly or explicitly, policy makers too frequently design policies based on the assumption that individuals will pursue their own self-interest (Taylor-Gooby, 1998; 2000).

Starting at the level of the household, then, allows us to critique materialist values. Commentators have always been aware of a more humanist agenda underlying Marx's "scientific socialism", one that has the potential to take Marxism away from narrowly economistic concerns. The well-being of people living in households does not derive from money income alone. A Marxist paradigm integrates work activity into the development of the whole human being; for whilst it is true that most of Marx's economic analysis is concerned with capitalist development as a process of creating material wealth, Marx was also anxious to ask how material wealth becomes *real* wealth through the all-sided and full development of each individual. Marx's analysis of the commoditisation of time in the historical evolution of capitalism allows us to understand how gendered constraints on the achievement of household well-being can come about.

On the basis of Marx's analysis, Julkunen (1977) suggests that the process of economic development involves the development of a sense of time, with the capitalist economy as the first economy of conscious time saving. The paradox is that, with more highly developed productive resources, time becomes relatively more expensive and valuable; so that the more time is saved, the scarcer it becomes. As we shall see, the political and economic conditions of the last 25 years have allowed the labour/time-saving compulsion of competitive capitalism to be off-loaded on to households in the form of a (gender differentiated) increase in commoditised time spent on income earning. As ever more women join men in the labour market, how far does this mean that the material wealth of households has grown at the expense of other forms of well-being; those deriving, for example, from unpaid work? As Julkunen would see it, the full development of human activity is only possible if:

> ... both the society as a whole and the individuals within it allocate time in the right proportions to all activities, not simply in terms of paid working time, but of the entire time fund of the society and the individual. (Wheelock, 1990a, pp. 128-129)

Household level research provides an opportunity to find out how the formal (paid) economy and the complementary economy of unpaid work interact with each other; for livelihoods involve a jigsaw puzzle, which may include pieces of waged work, self employment, unpaid domestic and caring work, state transfers and so on (Smith & Wallerstein, 1992). A restructuring economy changes livelihoods and leads to gendered shifts between market, state and household-based sources (as in the case of the unemployed men with employed wives mentioned above). An interdisciplinary approach is essential to understanding this kind of household change and its impact on the well-being of people's lives. One of the classic founders of socio-economics is Karl Polanyi, and his *The Great Transformation* (1944), published near the end of the Second World War, theorises the effects of the growth of the market economy since the beginning of the nineteenth century. Polanyi argues forcefully about the changing way in which the market is successively embedded in, and disembedded from, social and cultural institutions. He is particularly concerned to analyse the impact of an economic system - as he sees it, unique in human history - that is founded on the pursuit of personal economic gain. Polanyi himself shows no awareness of gender in his analysis of the damage that marketisation can inflict on established patterns of social relations and cultural institutions or the protective responses that this brings forth from the groups affected (Waller & Jennings, 1991). However, a Polanyian research agenda certainly involves studying the ways in which people's lives are structured by changing livelihoods (Stanfield, 1986) and household level research and analysis allows gender to be integrated into such an agenda.

Karl Polanyi has in recent years provided me with as much inspiration as Marx had done in my more abstract theoretical days. How can the changes to the capitalist market economy since Polanyi published his work in 1944 be characterised? How have they structured the interactions between non-commoditised, commoditised and state-based economic relations in the household? What has been the effect on well-being and wealth in its broadest sense? How have policies that relate to people's household lives impacted on gender relations? At the risk of oversimplifying, the major shift in household livelihoods has been from reliance upon a family *wage* to reliance upon family *employment*,[3] as the economy has shifted from a regime of security during the long post-war boom to one of insecurity (Wheelock, 1999a), from a Keynesian welfare state to a Schumpeterian workfare state (Jessop, 1994). Like Becker's household, the policy makers' family wage model of the post-war years - inherited from decades of (male) trade union struggle during the nineteenth and twentieth centuries - assumed a single utility function for the household. This was a model that hid gender imbalances inside the household. With a regulated Fordist labour

---

[3] This can also take the form of family self-employment or small business activity (Baines & Wheelock, 1998).

market, Keynesian demand management, decommoditised health and education, and a benefits regime based on lifetime redistribution via an insurance-based system, a male breadwinner could be relied upon to be financially responsible for the members of his household. Traditional gender roles meant that caring was undertaken by wives inside that household. The welfare state remained largely outside the front door, leaving the individuals within to manage the financial dependence of wives and the domestic dependence of husbands in whatever way they saw fit, and security for women was largely dependent upon marriage to a breadwinner (Wheelock, Oughton & Baines, 2003).

Over the following decades, this gendered model came under increasing strain. More insecure labour markets, the abandonment of Keynesian employment policies, the shift to means-tested welfare benefits, aspirations for higher living standards and the new wave of women's liberation mentioned at the start of this chapter meant a shift to *family* employment for more and more households (Wheelock, 1999b). Generally, this involved *part-time* employment for women, bringing in a component wage while enabling mothers to retain their traditional domestic and caring roles (Humphries & Rubery, 1992). This gave wives only a *constrained* financial independence, partly because of the low wages and poor labour market conditions that women are particularly subject to, but also because households tended to consider any childcare costs as a deduction from *women's* wages, rather than from *household* income. Unsurprisingly, with growing rates of family breakdown, women and children became much more subject to poverty and insecurity. Men continued to be domestically dependent.

Feminist research of the 1980s and 1990s demonstrated that it was largely women who were proving flexible in relation to changing economic and policy circumstances (e.g. Bruegel, Figart & Mutari, 1998). Policy models associated with the shift to family employment paid some attention to gender issues, for example with family friendly employment policies; but the potentially devastating and destabilising impact on social reproduction - via pressure on women's time - was largely ignored (O'Hara, 1995). The family employment model meant longer hours at work for the family as a whole (Schor, 1992); and what did this mean for household well-being, especially for the care of children, or indeed the elderly and the sick? Marx does not just explain why capitalism increases the time pressure on some households; his humanist agenda also demands that we look beyond economistic conceptions of "wealth" to ways of promoting household well-being.

Although the family employment model was the most common development after the long post-war boom ended, a further contrasting model became increasingly common: the long-term benefits-dependent household.[4] Two different tendencies gave rise to this. Firstly, there were increasing rates of family breakdown, owing to divorce and separation. Secondly, labour market and benefit changes meant that many men were unable to earn a family wage, while at the same time it did not make sense for the *family* to earn, thanks to the difficulty of ensuring a regularly reliable income in the face of labour market insecurity (see Nelson & Smith, 1999, for the US situation). Again, there has been a tendency for policy to assume a single utility function for the household, staying outside the front door. It is the threat to the public purse

---

[4] This is very much in line with the Marxian conceptualisation that capitalism thrives on a reserve army of labour. It is, moreover, of no significance to capitalist society what the unemployed (or for that matter non-employed women) do with their time.

from benefit-dependent households that successive governments, including New Labour, have sought to tackle. In its concern to "make work pay", the Labour government has identified childcare as a macro-economic issue which, if made affordable, could move both two-parent and one-parent households into family employment. In this model, social policy again tends to stay outside the front door, merely *modifying* traditional gendered caring roles by implicitly delivering state additions to childcare to *mothers* in particular, so relieving the pressure on their time (Wheelock & Jones, 2002).

Many of the changes just described have undermined the material basis for the patriarchal ideology that had found expression in the post-war gender order. Yet, with their partners increasingly employed in the labour market, men have only marginally increased their participation in unpaid work at home (Anderson, Bechhofer & Gershuny, 1994). This "lagged response" of the domestic division of labour to labour market change seems likely to exacerbate social trends towards higher divorce and separation rates, as women find themselves increasingly bearing the costs of providing material and emotional security for themselves and their children, regardless of whether they are living with a partner or not.

So how sustainable is the family employment model under a regime of insecurity? The current situation looks set to undermine it. Firstly, the family employment model has underpinned and reinforced the labour market and the income inequality that are features of the regime of insecurity (Bernstein, Mishel & Schmitt, 1998; Sennett, 1998). High-income men and women tend to be found as partners in the same households, and the same goes for low-income men and women. Folbre (1994, chap. 3) points to the danger that, if equal rights for women co-exist with continuing class and race inequalities, low-waged childcare and teaching will be done by men and women from disadvantaged groups. Secondly, labour market insecurity puts a premium on those who are prepared to " ... work all the hours that God sends".[5] Added pressures arise from the labour supply side, as more women enter the labour market. Men who are required to be present at work from early morning to late at night, or to work overtime, are not available to do the caring tasks and this makes it impracticable for many partners to undertake anything but part-time employment, while continuing to do the unpaid work at home (Bruegel, Figart & Mutari, 1998). This is just the kind of commoditisation of time that Marx analyses so effectively in Volume I of *Capital* (1912). But perhaps the greatest danger from the family employment model lies in the ways in which it threatens to undermine social reproduction. Fertility rates provide an indicator: the average age at which women have their first child is now at a historical high, the same age as it was in the aftermath of the First World War. The threats to household stability from long hours are bad enough (recently made worse by the chaos brought about by the marketisation of the railways and consequent extensions to commuting time), but it is above all the likely deficit in the care available for our children that needs to be taken seriously (Purdy, 1998).

But is this not just scaremongering? I started this chapter by mentioning the National Childcare Strategy, which recognises that childcare is a macroeconomic issue, not simply a matter for individual households to sort out. Childcare is deemed to be important for its own sake, because of the benefits it gives to children in terms of counteracting social exclusion, and in supporting women

---

[5] This was a phrase used by one of the unemployed men I interviewed to refer to how hard he had worked right up to the moment of his redundancy in the early 1980s.

(*sic*) in going back to work. The strategy should bring Britain's childcare provision more into line with that of other European economies. The approach is essentially that of a tax-credit-primed, market provision, in which childcare quality is underpinned by an inspection and accreditation regime. Underlying this regulated market approach to childcare is an implicit assumption of the economic behavioural model: that people take individualist, cost-benefit type decisions about how to maximise personal gain. But are people's choices about childcare actually made in response to purely financial incentives, and will childcare that is being conceived of as a final (albeit regulated and subsidised) market frontier actually work?

In the 1990s, feminist analysis began to distinguish between domestic and caring work, focusing theoretical analysis on developing an understanding of caring. Nancy Folbre's *Who Cares for the Kids?* (1994) led the way in proposing that "structures of constraint" could provide a conceptual framework with which to identify the distribution of the costs of social reproduction, thereby addressing an issue that economics had traditionally turned its back upon. Sue Himmelweit (1995) revisited the earlier ideas of the domestic labour debate, that paid and unpaid work should receive parity of theoretical treatment. She suggested that caring should perhaps not be viewed as work, because caring cannot be separated from the personal relationship (of parenting, say), while the market is based on a depersonalised commodification of work. Putting it starkly, can we be paid to care? Alex Howard (1996), for example, has shown that, when it comes to counselling, it is both philosophically and practically problematic to answer such a question in the affirmative.

One of my most recent pieces of empirical work confirms the problems that can arise for policies relating to caring work. In its laudable objective to provide a choice of high quality affordable and accessible childcare to parents, the Department for Education and Employment has not yet asked local childcare partnerships to take into account the substantial volume of informal or complementary childcare provided - usually without money changing hands - by grandparents and other relatives, friends or neighbours.[6] In investigating complementary childcare in North-East England, it became apparent that - with market and welfare state failures - the family employment model was being extensively underpinned by the (unpaid) provision of childcare by grandparents (Wheelock & Jones, 2002). Time pressures from the capitalist market economy are, in other words, being relieved through the complementary economy. On the one hand, this study showed that parents - particularly mothers - were not happy for childcare to be provided *only* through the market when they themselves were out at work. With the well-being of themselves, their children and the grandparents in mind, they often saw "grandparents as the next best thing". On the other hand, complementary childcare also appeared to have a strong tendency to reproduce gendered patterns of care across the generations, for it was predominantly grand*mothers* who were making a gift of (gendered) caring time to their daughters (Sirianni & Negrey, 2000).

In terms of national income per head, we are far richer than we were 25 years ago. However, the shift to family employment, the requirement for the middle classes to be present for long hours at work ("presentism"), and the low wages being paid to the rest, mean both that all households are working longer hours, and that there is much greater

---

[6] As of 2003, it would appear that the newly-formed SureStart Unit is paying some attention to this issue.

inequality of income than there was then (see Wilkinson, 1996, for the socially and economically destructive impact of inequality). There are, then, doubts about how far the living standards of (healthy) adults have risen in the last quarter of a century. Those in need of care - and particularly children - may well be much worse off. If policies for work-life balance are to have an impact, we must return to Marxian concerns with the impact of the commoditisation of time and to Polanyi's anxieties about extending market relations. Do we really want to purchase more care in a market setting? It is more likely that increased well-being can come only from a radical programme for the redistribution of work, which then gives all households the choice of working shorter hours, rather than seeking higher incomes (Wheelock & Vail, 1998). It is this kind of balance between work and life that Marx - in his *Economic and Philosophical Manuscripts* (1970/1959) - and Polanyi (1944) were concerned with. For leading a characteristically *human* life is surely about men having time for their children, as well as women having time in the workplace.

*References*

Anderson M., Bechhofer F., & Gershuny J. (Eds.) (1994). *The social and political economy of the household.* New York: Oxford University Press.

Baines, S., & Wheelock, J. (1998). Reinventing traditional solutions: Job creation, gender and the micro-business household. *Work, Employment and Society,* 12 (4), 579-601.

Becker, G. (1980). A theory of the allocation of time. In A. H. Amsden (Ed.), *The economics of women and work* (pp. 52-81). Harmondsworth: Penguin. (Original work published 1965).

Bell, C., & McKee, L. (1985). Marital and family relations in times of male unemployment. In B. Roberts, R. Finnegan, & D. Gallie (Eds.), *New approaches to economic life: Economic restructuring: Employment and the social division of labour* (pp. 387-399). Manchester: Manchester University Press.

Bernstein, J., Mishel, L., & Schmitt, J. (1998). The US model: the wages of inequality. In J. Wheelock & J. Vail (Eds.), *Work and idleness: The political economy of full employment* (pp. 157-182). Boston: Kluwer Academic.

Bruegel, I., Figart, D., & Mutari, E. (1998). Whose full employment?: A feminist perspective on work redistribution. In J. Wheelock & J. Vail (Eds.), *Work and idleness: The political economy of full employment* (pp. 69-83). Boston: Kluwer Academic.

Cockburn, C. (1983). *Brothers: Male dominance and technological change.* London: Pluto Press.

Crompton, R., Jones, G., & Reid, S. (1982). Contemporary clerical work: A study of local government. In J. West

(Ed.), *Work, women and the labour market* (pp. 44-60). London: Routledge & Kegan Paul.

Dunleavy, P. (1991). *Democracy, bureaucracy and public choice: Economic explanations in political science.* London: Harvester.

Elster, J. (1985). *Making sense of Marx.* Cambridge: Cambridge University Press.

Engels, F. (1940). *The origin of the family, private property and the state* (A. West & D. Torr, Trans.). London: Lawrence & Wishart. (Original work published 1884).

Equal Pay Act: Elizabeth II, 1970, Chapter 41 (1970). London, HMSO.

Folbre, N. (1994). *Who pays for the kids?: Gender and the structures of constraint.* London: Routledge.

Gregson, N., & Lowe, M. (1993). Renegotiating the domestic division of labour?: A study of dual career families in north east and south east England. *The Sociological Review, 41,* 475-505.

Himmelweit, S. (1995). The discovery of "unpaid work": The consequences of the expansion of "work". *Feminist Economics, 1* (2), 1-19.

Himmelweit, S. (Ed.) (2000). *Inside the household: From labour to care.* Basingstoke: Macmillan.

Howard, A. (1996). *Challenges to counselling and psychotherapy.* London: Macmillan.

Humphries, J., & Rubery, J. (1992). The legacy for women's employment: Integration, differentiation and polarisation. In J. Michie (Ed.), *The economic legacy 1979-1992* (pp. 236-254). London: Academic Press.

Jessop, B. (1994). The transition to post-Fordism and the Schumpeterian workfare state. In R. Burrows and B. Loader (Eds.), *Towards a post-Fordist welfare state?* (pp. 13-39). London: Routledge.

Julkunen, R. (1977). A contribution to the categories of social time and the economy of time. *Acta Sociologica, 20* (1), 1-15.

Marx, K. (1912). *Capital: A critical analysis of capitalist production* (S. Moore & E. Aveling, Trans.). London: Glaisher. (Original work published 1867, 1885, 1894).

Marx, K. (1970). *Economic and philosophical manuscripts of 1844* (D. J. Struik, Ed.; M. Milligan, Trans.). London: Lawrence and Wishart. (Original work published 1959).

Morris, L. (1985). Renegotiation of the domestic division of labour in the context of redundancy. In B. Roberts, R. Finnegan & D. Gallie (Eds.), *New approaches to economic life* (pp. 400-416). Manchester: Manchester University Press.

Nelson, M. K., & Smith, J. (1999). *Working hard and making do: Surviving in small town America.* Berkeley: University of California Press.

Oakley, A. (1974). *The sociology of housework.* Oxford: Martin Robertson.

O'Hara, P. A. (1995). Household labour, the family and macroeconomic stability in the US, 1940s to 1990. *Review of Social Economy, 53*(1), 89-120.

Polanyi, K. (1944). *The great transformation: The political and economic origins of our time.* New York: Farrar & Rinehart.

Porter, M. (1982). Standing on the edge: Working class housewives and the world of work. In J. West (Ed.), *Work, women and the labour market* (pp. 117-134). London: Routledge & Kegan Paul.

Purdy, D. (1998). Redistributing work: the role of the welfare state. In J. Wheelock & J. Vail (Eds.), *Work and idleness: The political economy of full employment* (pp. 205-218). Boston: Kluwer Academic.

Roemer, J. (Ed.) (1986). *Analytical Marxism.* Cambridge: Cambridge University Press.

Schor, J. B. (1992). *The overworked American: The unexpected decline of leisure.* New York: Basic Books.

Sennett, R. (1998). *The corrosion of character: The personal consequences of work in the new capitalism.* New York: Norton.

Sirianni, C., & Negrey, C. (2000). Working time as gendered time. *Feminist Economics, 6*(1), 59-76.

Smith, J., & Wallerstein, I. (1992). *Creating and transforming households: The constraints of the world economy.* Cambridge: Cambridge University Press.

Stanfield, J. R. (1986). *The economic thought of Karl Polanyi: Lives and livelihood.* Basingstoke: Macmillan.

Stubbs, C., & Wheelock, J. (1990). *A women's work in the changing local economy.* Aldershot: Avebury.

Taylor-Gooby, P. (Ed.) (1998). *Choice and public policy: The limitations to welfare markets.* Basingstoke: Macmillan.

Taylor-Gooby, P. (Ed.) (2000). *Risk, trust and welfare.* Basingstoke: Macmillan.

Wajcman, J. (1983). *Women in control: Dilemmas of a workers' co-operative.* Milton Keynes: Open University Press.

Waller, W., & Jennings, A. (1991). A feminist institutionalist reconsideration of Karl Polanyi. *Journal of Economic Issues, 25* (2), 485-497.

Wheelock, J. (1990a). Capital restructuring and the domestic economy: Family self respect and the irrelevance of "rational economic man". *Capital and Class, 41,* 103-141.

Wheelock, J. (1990b). *Husbands at home: The domestic economy in a post-industrial economy.* London: Routledge.

Wheelock, J. (1999a). Who dreams of failure?: Insecurity in modern capitalism. In J. Vail, J. Wheelock & M. Hill (Eds.), *Insecure times: Living with insecurity in contemporary society* (pp. 23-40). London: Routledge.

Wheelock, J. (1999b). Fear or opportunity?: Insecurity in employment. In J. Vail, J. Wheelock & M. Hill (Eds.), *Insecure times: Living with insecurity in contemporary society* (pp. 75-88). London: Routledge.

Wheelock, J., & Jones, K. (2002). "Grandparents are the next best thing": Informal childcare for working parents in urban Britain. *Journal of Social Policy, 31* (3), 441-463.

Wheelock, J, & Oughton, E. (1996). The household as a focus for research. *Journal of Economic Issues.* 30 (1), 143-159.

Wheelock, J., Oughton, E., & Baines, S. (2003). Getting by with a little help from your family: Toward a policy-relevant model of the household. *Feminist Economics, 9* (1), 19-45.

Wheelock, J., & Vail J. (Eds.). (1998). *Work and idleness: The political economy of full employment.* Boston: Kluwer Academic.

Wilkinson, R. (1996). *Unhealthy societies: The afflictions of inequality.* London: Routledge.

Yeandle, S. (1984). *Women's working lives: Patterns and strategies*. London: Tavistock.

Yi, Y.-A. (1996). Margaret G. Reid: life and achievements. *Feminist Economics, 2* (3), 17-36.

# 8

# APPROACHES TO GENDER AND DEVELOPMENT: PERSPECTIVES FROM URBAN MEXICO

## Katie Willis

*Introduction*

Debates rage about "development", particularly about what policies should be implemented to achieve it; (for overviews, see, for example: Allen & Thomas, 2000; Hettne, 1995; Potter, Binns, Elliott & Smith, 1999; Simon & Närman, 1999). However, less attention is often given to what is actually meant by "development" and to a recognition that, in reality, development is a dynamic process rather than an end point per se. Within the vast amount of material on development, three key strands can be identified as being crucial to how development is conceived (either explicitly or implicitly): improvements in standards of living; improvements in quality of life; and greater equity and justice. Different indicators may be used to measure these "goals" and there is disagreement regarding which policies will bring about these positive changes, but these factors lie at the heart of what development is about.

In this paper, I consider one factor which cross-cuts the development debate: how does gender affect our conceptions of what "development" is and how it can be achieved? Policies aimed at improving living standards often have gendered outcomes, and indicators of "quality of life" may differ between men and women, just as they do between different age groups, ethnic groups, etc.

## Approaches to Gender and Development

Following a section that discusses the changing approaches to gender and development, the paper moves on to focus on Mexico as a case study. Development trajectories and gender ideologies are clearly time and place specific, so a focus on one country will help us to understand the complexity of the processes taking place. Within the Mexican context, I highlight the impact of macro-economic development policies on employment structures and intra-household activities, stressing both the gendered dimensions, but also the cleavages within the category "woman". Not all women experience and are affected by policies in the same way. The paper concludes with a discussion of how men have been and should be explicitly incorporated into development policies *as* men, rather than as ungendered beings. This opens up the possibilities of examining the fluidity of gender roles and relations, while recognising some fixity within a broadly patriarchal system.

*Why should we consider Gender in Development Strategies?*

Approaches to development, both in theory terms and in policy/practice terms, have changed greatly since the Second World War (Närman, 1999). Increasingly, the diversity of populations is recognised, with an awareness that, because of this diversity, a "one size fits all" strategy is not appropriate. It is only really since the 1970s that development theory and development policy-makers have started to consider in depth the ways in which gender (i.e. social differences between men and women) has an impact on the effectiveness and nature of development (see Pearson, 2000, for overview).

International agencies, such as the United Nations organisations and non-governmental organisations [NGOs] have taken on board the gender dimension and have increasingly promoted "gender-aware" policies, sometimes setting up specific "gender units" to deal with issues of gender inequality. The United Nations Development Program [UNDP], which deals with "social development" issues (i.e. looking at development beyond the purely economic aspects), now includes gender-specific information within its annual *Human Development Report*. It also includes a composite measure, the Gender-Related Development Index [GDI], to highlight how national-level statistics on the standard and quality of life may differ once the effects on women and men have been considered separately. The GDI is based on the Human Development Index [HDI], which is a composite measure based on figures for life expectancy, education and national economic performance.

Caroline Moser has been one of the most high-profile researchers in highlighting the gendered nature of development strategies. She has identified a number of approaches adopted by governments and development agencies in dealing with gender in development policies. These approaches are, however, usually focused on women rather than men, a factor that affects our understanding of both the gendered nature of development and of policy effectiveness (Moser, 1993).

Moser identifies five main approaches to women and development, but I will only pick up on three of them in this paper, to exemplify gender and development approaches in Mexico. The first is the "welfare approach", which constructs and treats women as victims who need to be helped, rather than capable actors in their own right. In addition, policies under this heading deal with women as wives and mothers, and therefore within the domestic realm, rather than in relation to wider issues, such as paid employment. Secondly, Moser's "efficiency approach" category, which involves policies which view women as able to undertake paid work and suggests that development can be achieved more effectively if all members of the population are involved. Finally, the most recent development is the so-called "empowerment" approach, dealing with issues of equity and power.

According to Moser, therefore, the reasons women have over time been a particular focus of development policies could be because: (a) women are regarded as the most disadvantaged group in society and therefore in need of help; (b) involving women makes "development" more efficient; and (c) focusing attention on women helps promote gender equity and human rights for all. Of course, notions of "progress" and "equity" are contested concepts and it could be argued that the whole construction of "gender equity" is a Northern Eurocentric concept. This means that the gender and development debate is fraught with contradictions and difficulties. This paper aims to highlight some of these problems within the Mexican urban context.

*Gender Relations in Mexico*

In any discussion of gender and development, the context of the theorising or the policy development should be considered. While, globally, there is an overall tendency for women to be disadvantaged relative to men, the nature of this disadvantage varies (see, for example, Brydon & Chant, 1989; Momsen & Townsend, 1987). If gender equity is the aim of policy-making, then the specific social, political and economic context must be acknowledged and policies tailored as appropriate.

In Mexico, as in much of Latin America, the starting point for a discussion of gender relations is often what has been termed the *machismo/marianismo* model (Stevens, 1973). This is a form of patriarchy within which men are expected to be the heads of households, breadwinners and those involved in the public sphere. In contrast, women's roles are constructed as being those within the domestic environment, focusing on childcare and housework. In addition, men's public roles involve non-censure for drunkenness and violence, and having multiple sexual partners, even when married, is supposedly not frowned upon. For women, chastity and demure behaviour are regarded as imperative, to maintain family honour.

This model is, however, very rigid and, while providing a useful starting point for a consideration of gender relations in Latin America, it does not help in describing and explaining the real-life experiences of men and women. It is also not very useful from a policy development point of view. What a great deal of research has demonstrated is that gender relations are fluid, both spatially and temporally, as they are socially constructed, rather than a reflection of innate biological characteristics (see, for example, Ehlers, 1991; Gutmann, 1996). In practical terms, this means that policies may have positive or negative outcomes, but it also means that sensitive policy implementation will be characterised by intense negotiation and an awareness of a range of specificities.

Despite this fluidity, women as a group are disadvantaged relative to men both nationally and at regional and local levels when a number of key indicators are examined (Table 1). In 1999, Mexico had a Human Development Index of 0.790 which ranked the country 51st in the world (UNDP, 2001, p.146); but, when this was adjusted to take gender into account, the GDI figure was 0.782 and the ranking 49th (UNDP, 2001, p.211). For Mexico, taking gender differences into account lowered the index, so demonstrating female disadvantage; but this higher ranking also shows that countries with initially higher HDI figures could slip down the table when gender inequalities were taken into account.

Table 1: Gender Differences in Key Indicators, Mexico

|  | Women | Men |
|---|---|---|
| Adult Literacy Rates (2000)[1] | 88.7 | 92.6 |
| Labour Force Participation (2000)[2] | 36.4 | 76.8 |
| Political Participation (2000)[3] | 15.6 (Senate) 16.0 (Chamber of Deputies) | 84.4 (Senate) 84.0 (Chamber of Deputies) |

[1] For population aged 15 and over. Instituto Nacional de Estadística Geografía e Informática [INEGI] (2002, p.226)
[2] For population aged 12 and over. INEGI (2002, p.318)
[3] INEGI (2002, pp. 409-410)

At a national scale, therefore, it appears that Mexican "women" as a group are disadvantaged relative to Mexican "men" as a group. This does not mean that *all* women are in a less privileged and more marginal position than *all* men, but there are clearly structural factors that need to be considered when examining the impact of development policies.

*Mexico: Development Issues*

Having outlined the key features of gender relations within Mexico, it is important to highlight the main development features and policies, as these will both reflect and affect women's and men's experiences within Mexican cities. Gender is clearly important when considering rural development in Mexico (see, for example, Stephen, 1991; Townsend, Zapata, Rowlands, Alberti & Mercado, 1999), but, given the limitations of space, of my own research experience and the fact that, in 1999, 74.2% of the Mexican population lived in urban areas (UNDP, 2001, p. 155), I have decided to focus on towns and cities in this paper.

In the post-Second World War period, Mexico experienced what has been termed the "Mexican Miracle", with rapid levels of economic growth and decreasing levels of poverty. A key element of this period was import-substitution industrialisation [ISI], by which the Mexican government supported local companies to produce industrial goods, rather than importing them. Government policies included subsidies and a tariff system that made domestically produced goods cheaper (Barry, 1992). However, by the late 1970s the national economy was in trouble. The national government had borrowed heavily from international banks to finance its earlier development policies, relying on low interest rates, a buoyant international economy and continuing domestic economic success. In the later 1970s, this situation became increasingly problematic, as national-level growth slowed down, with the limits of import-substitution becoming very apparent, the global economy also slowing down and rapid rises in oil prices and in interest rates at the international level. All these factors meant that the Mexican government could not meet the interest payments on its loans and in 1982 the government was forced to default, so heralding the arrival of the "debt crisis" and the "lost decade" for many Latin American and African nations (Green, 1995; Roddick, 1988).

Structural adjustments policies [SAPs] were implemented in Mexico, as elsewhere, in an attempt to stabilise the economy and to provide sustainable growth, in economic terms. These SAPs were endorsed by the International Monetary Fund [IMF] and the World Bank, which both had a particular neo-liberal view of "development", focusing on the role of the market as the provider and the state as a "facilitator". Without endorsement from these international financial institutions, countries were unable to gain further loans, either from the IMF, the World Bank or from international private banks and governments (Stewart, 1995).

Under SAPs, governments were expected to reduce expenditure and maximise income. Expenditure reduction involved policies such as laying off large numbers of state employees and reducing subsidies for food, health, education and other vital services. State enterprises, such as the telecommunications company Telmex, were privatised and the economy was opened up to greater foreign investment (Green, 1995).

While such policies did stabilise the economy to some degree and allowed the Mexican government access to loans (although there was another period of extreme economic crisis in 1994-95; see Table 2), it clearly did not have a beneficial effect on all members of the Mexican population. According to UNDP (2000), 17.9% of the Mexican population lived on less than $1 per day in the period 1989-1998. Income inequality is very marked within Mexico and there are suggestions that this inequality increased throughout the 1980s and 1990s (Tello, 1991). The poorest 20% have 3.6% of the wealth, while the top 20% have 58.2% of the wealth (UNDP, 2000).

Table 2: Economic and Social Development Indicators, Mexico

|      | GDP per capita (1995 US$)[1] | HDI[2] |
|------|------------------------------|--------|
| 1975 | 3,380                        | 0.688  |
| 980  | 4,167                        | 0.732  |
| 1985 | 4,106                        | 0.750  |
|      | 046                          | 759    |
| 1995 | -                            | 0.772  |
| 1998 | 4,459                        | 0.784[2] |
| 1999 | -                            | 0.790  |

[1] UNDP (2000, p.179)
[2] UNDP (2001, p.146)

Under these conditions, the need for cooperation between individuals to try to get through these problems was paramount. The notion of "household survival strategies" has often been used in this situation to describe how different members of a household work together (Murphy & Stepick, 1991; Samarasinghe, 1997; Selby, Murphy & Lorenzen, 1990). Individuals have different skills and resources, based on gender, age, employment, education, etc. For individuals, such resources may not enable daily survival; but when individuals work together and pool their resources, "getting by" may at least be possible. Gender will be a key variable within the household, reflecting different skills, and also the power relations within the household and wider society, and gender norms in relation to work (both paid and unpaid).

## Approaches to Gender and Development

### Women in the Work Force: Informal Sector Activities

One of the key areas of response to the changing economy is shifts in employment – as people are laid off or as the labour market becomes more "flexible", to serve the interests of capital, there is a need for greater income generation within the household. Men who worked previously may be employed in more than one job and people who did not have paid employment, e.g. children and women, may go into the labour force.

Within Latin America, there is some debate about the extent to which the economic crisis led to greater numbers of women going into the labour force. Censuses and labour force survey material show the increasing participation of women in the Mexican labour force long before the 1980s, reflecting women's increasing education levels and changing attitudes to women's involvement in paid work (see Table 3). However, there is no doubt of the importance of women's involvement in income generation and also of the fact that small-scale surveys refer to women who claim that they are in paid work because of economic pressures in the household (see, for example, Chant, 1990, 1994). These pressures are not only experienced by economically poorer, "working-class", households, but also by middle-class households which had benefited most from the widespread activities of the Mexican state (see Escobar Latapí & Roberts, 1991; Willis, 2000).

Many Mexicans work in what has been termed "the informal sector". While the boundaries of such a sector are difficult to define, such activities are unregulated by the state, tend to lack job security and pay wages that are often low and irregular (McIlwaine, Chant & Lloyd-Evans, 2002; Potter & Lloyd-Evans, 1998; Thomas, 1995). The diversity of figures in Table 3 reflects the problems of defining the

## Table 3: Mexican Labour Force Participation Rates by Gender (Population Aged 12 and Over)

|  | Women (%) | Men (%) | TOTAL (%) |
|---|---|---|---|
| **Census 1950** | 13.06 | 88.03 | 49.39 |
| **Census 1960** | 18.19 | 85.66 | 51.41 |
| **Census 1970** | 17.61 | 70.12 | 43.47 |
| **Census 1980** | 27.75 | 75.05 | 50.91 |
| **National Employment Survey 1988** | 32.33 | 75.35 | 53.19 |
| **Census 1990** | 19.58 | 68.01 | 43.04 |
| **National Employment Survey 1991** | 31.48 | 77.74 | 53.55 |
| **National Employment Survey 2000[1]** | 36.4 | 76.8 | - |

Source: Jusidman & Eternod (1994, p.8), except [1] (INEGI, 2002, p.318).

"informal sector" and also of collecting information on individuals involved in such activities.

Labour market segmentation by gender is clearly evident within the informal sector, with women concentrated in activities such as street trading and domestic service, while men are more likely to work in construction and associated activities, transport and also commerce. In general, women are more likely than men to be found in informal sector occupations, reflecting differences in education levels, gendered jobs and the greater flexibility of many informal sector occupations, which thus allow women with domestic responsibilities to combine these activities with remunerated ones (Willis, 1996).

For example, in my 1992 survey of 100 households in an informal settlement on the outskirts of Oaxaca City, Southern Mexico, while the vast majority of adults in paid employment worked in the informal sector, there was a significant gender division: 81.7% of male heads of household had informal jobs, while the figure for women heads of household (either sole head, or joint head) was 90.6%. Differential incorporation into the labour force can be a reflection of choice on the part of workers or it can reflect a lack of choice, with employers channelling workers with particular characteristics into certain jobs; or it can reflect the social construction of some forms of employment as being only suitable for some workers – defined in relation to gender, age, marital status and ethnicity, for example. In Mexico, it is legal to have job advertisements specifying gender, age, marital status, religion and even appearance.

## Women in the Work Force: Multinational Corporation Employment

Although women may be disproportionately found in the informal sector overall, many women do work in the "formal" sector, in both the state system (e.g. in health, education and the bureaucracy) and the private sector. One of the most well known areas of employment in the latter is multinational corporation [MNC] assembly factory employment.

Assembly factories (also known as *maquilas* or *maquiladoras* in Mexico) have been a feature of the

Northern Mexican economy and landscape since the 1950s and 1960s. In particular, the Border Industrialisation Programme [BIP] was implemented from 1965 by the Mexican Government to create employment for local men. In the post-Second World War period, thousands of Mexican men had legally travelled to the USA to work in agriculture, under the Bracero Programme. However, this programme came to an end in the early 1960s, leaving a severe employment shortage. The BIP aimed to attract foreign investment to the northern border region to replace these agricultural jobs (Kopinak, 1997). However, while jobs were created, the vast majority were for women. This process continued following the massive growth in *maquilas*, which was linked to Mexico's entry into the North American Free Trade Agreement [NAFTA] on 1 January 1994. The foci of this activity are in the border cities, such as Ciudad Juarez, Matamoros and Tijuana.

By 2000, the number of *maquila* plants in Mexico stood at 3,703, employing approximately 1.3 million workers (INEGI, cited in Maquila Portal, 2002) and producing 98.79 billion US dollars worth of goods (Ciemez-Vefa, cited in Maquila Portal, 2002). More recent figures reflect global economic problems and the shifting of production from Mexico to cheaper locations in East Asia, but as of November 2001 there were still 3,527 *maquila* plants in Mexico (INEGI, cited in Maquila Portal, 2002).

The predominance of women in these factories matches that found in free trade zones in other parts of the world, such as the Caribbean and South-East Asia (Chant & McIlwaine, 1995; Lim, 1990; Safa, 1995). Women are often preferred by employers because of essentialist notions about women being nimble-fingered, passive and more reliable than men, as well as for the fact that women can be paid less than men, for a variety of broader gender norms in society. However, it is important to recognise that, while women are concentrated on the factory floor, management positions are male-dominated (although for an exception, see Wright, 1997). In addition, men are increasingly entering factory employment, particularly in sectors that are regarded as "male", such as those in which heavy machinery is used (Cantanzarite & Strober, 1993; Pearson, 1995).

The process of labour recruitment is not, however, gendered in a very simple way; rather, the preference for male or female labour is also refined, with demands for particular "kinds" of female labour, drawing on assumptions regarding age and marital status. In many factories, young unmarried women are preferred, because employers perceive these women as being less militant, more reliable because of their supposed lack of domestic responsibilities, and cheaper, even though they will tend to have higher levels of education than their older counterparts (Cravey, 1998; Kopinak (1997).

María Patricia Fernández-Kelly (1997) provides a fascinating account of her experiences looking for work in a *maquila* in Ciudad Juarez. As part of her research into the impact of MNC employment on women's lives, she applied for jobs in the textile and garment sector. She describes how security guards or secretaries would often tell her that there were no jobs available, perhaps because she was over twenty-five. Not being part of local networks also hindered her job opportunities, as employers often prefer to hire workers through existing employees, so as to reduce the potential for "trouble-making". When Fernández-Kelly asked questions about her contract, hours of work and other employment conditions, employers were often wary, seeing her behaviour as undesirable. Before being hired, she was sent for a "medical test", which was really a pregnancy test, as the company did not want to hire pregnant women. Once hired, she describes the working conditions, particularly the pressures to complete the daily production quota. Despite the problems, Fernández-Kelly does describe some of the camaraderie between the women, particularly outside the factory, in the clubs and bars of the city.

This example demonstrates how national and local development strategies are gendered. Capitalism, in this case represented by MNCs that have located their factories in Mexico, is intertwined with local gender norms and expectations. In a later section, I shall examine the question of whether such gendered employment practices can destabilise pre-existing gender relations, or whether hierarchies of power are re-inscribed through the operation of multinational capital.

*Domestic Labour – Reproducing the Labour Force*

As well as monetary income, households also need to be "reproduced" in order to survive. "Reproduction" encompasses not only biological reproduction, but also the day-to-day physical reproduction of household members through the provision of food, shelter and clothing. The activities involved in providing this are largely female-dominated, because of the gender division of labour (see Moser, 1993). However, what becomes very clear is that the balance of work between men and women does not shift, even when women are in paid employment: i.e. they work what is called a "double day".

Large amounts of research have demonstrated that SAPs tend to create more domestic work, as women have to look for cheaper food or make the food they do have last longer, etc. (for example, González de la Rocha, 1988, 1994). There is also increased home production of food and clothing. An example taken from my work in Oaxaca City can be used to exemplify some of these processes. The

Martinez family (not their real name) lives in a corrugated iron dwelling on a steep hillside to the north of the city. Maria is a domestic servant, her husband is a carpenter and the five children do a variety of informal jobs, as well as going to school. Maria goes to work at about 5.30 a.m. every day and cleans for a number of families in the city centre. She returns at about 7 p.m., having completed her day's paid work, but also having scoured the city centre markets for cheap food. The children help out, for example by buying tortillas from the local market and also by collecting water from the standpipe at the bottom of the hill, but the bulk of the housework is Maria's responsibility. She also raises chickens and grows maize on the plot. Her husband does not do any housework, even though his workshop is adjacent to the house and he is often present during the day.

In some households, an older woman (such as a grandmother) may take on these tasks, but obviously this depends on her physical condition, etc. In others, the eldest daughters may be mainly responsible for the housework, so affecting their ability to find paid work or to continue with their education. The gender distinction is still apparent within middle-class households (Willis, 2000). While these households can invariably afford to pay for domestic assistance, this paid assistance is almost always from another woman, so the maintenance of the household is reliant again on female labour. The activities of the domestic servants are usually regulated by the female head of the household, demonstrating that, while women may share their socially constructed positions of responsibility for domestic tasks, there are hierarchies of power between different groups of women (Chaney & García Castro, 1989).

Regardless of who is the main homemaker, it is clear that household survival is predicated on someone (in the vast majority of cases a woman) being able to take on the increasing domestic burden associated with SAPs and associated policies. This highlights what Diane Elson (1995) has termed "male bias in the development process". Macro-economic policy-makers either did not consider the impact of SAPs on domestic work burdens or they assumed that women were "idle" and therefore could easily take up the extra load. In fact, in the majority of cases, already overburdened women are given even more work to do. This reflects Moser's "efficiency" argument in relation to gender and development as outlined earlier.

*Issues of "Empowerment"*

This then brings us on to another dimension of the gender and development literature. Not only do we have to consider the ways in which women and men are involved in different activities and how these contribute to advances in household and national economic development, but we also have to consider issues of equity and quality of life.

The notion of "empowerment" is something that has seen a great deal of attention in the past ten years in development literature. It is associated with the increasing focus on "grassroots development" or "bottom-up" development, which means getting the people affected involved in decision-making, etc. and determining what they want (Karl, 1995). In gender terms, there is an understanding that "empowerment" means changes in prevailing gender relations, so that women have more of a say in their own lives. Rowlands (1997) highlights the diverse ways in which "power" can be conceived, stressing that there is more to power than "power over": i.e. the ability to get somebody else to do what you want. She stresses the importance of "power to", which is not about domination, but encompasses the potential to " ... create new possibilities" (p.13). This would involve a recognition that "the ways things are" is not necessarily "natural" or "given"; they are instead a product of social, economic and political processes and can, therefore, be challenged and changed. Other dimensions of power are "power with", which involves individuals working together to achieve a goal, and "power from within", referring to self-belief and self-esteem (see also Townsend et al., 1999).

"Empowerment" is clearly a diverse and contested concept, but one of the main themes in gender literature is the debate about the empowerment potential of paid employment for women. A common assumption is that when women have access to a wage, this will have a knock-on effect on their ability to make decisions (i.e. to have the power to do something about their own lives). In addition, involvement in a workplace can, it is argued, promote feelings of well-being and self-confidence, particularly through working alongside other women in similar positions (McClenaghan, 1997).

Empirical research demonstrates, however, that the route from employment to empowerment is certainly not a pre-given one and that development policies which aim to "empower" women through employment alone have very mixed outcomes. Two examples from my work in Oaxaca can be used to exemplify this. Claudia is a tortilla-maker and loves her job in the local market. She describes it as very tough in terms of the physical labour needed to carry large bags of maize and make the dough; also, having to get up early every day is very wearing. Spending hours in a smoky atmosphere can also be bad for one's health. However, she enjoys working in the market, interacting with other stall-holders and her customers. She is also delighted at the chance to generate her own income and reported that, despite economic problems, tortillas were such a staple food that, for many families, they were the only food item that continued to be purchased on a regular basis. When I first met Claudia in 1990, she was living with her husband, but things were not going well. On my return in 1992, she was living alone, after problems with her husband became too great. While clearly sad that the marriage had not worked, she was very positive about her ability to survive on her own income and continued to enjoy working in the market. While she may not use the term "empowerment", she clearly exhibits signs of finding paid work "empowering" in some senses.

In contrast, Teresa, who has the charcoal stall next to Claudia in the market, does not talk about her job in a way that could be interpreted as "empowerment". She started running the stall in the late 1980s because the family's income was becoming increasingly scarce and, as her children were old enough to look after themselves, she could leave the house to get paid work. A local market stall meant that she did not have to go far, but, when I asked her if she would prefer to be back at home, she looked at me amazed: why would anyone prefer the tiring work in the market to the domestic burden within the house? She said that she would give up her stall immediately if the household's financial situation improved. While she interacted with other stall-holders in the market and did not find the job isolating (unlike women who work in domestic service), Teresa's access to income and work outside the home was not interpreted by her in a positive way; rather, she saw it as a duty to her husband and children in times of need.

There are similar processes operating within MNC employment. While access to waged work is clearly beneficial for household maintenance, the working conditions and the burden of the "double day" can prove to be serious problems for women. Fernández-Kelly concludes that " ... *maquila* women would prefer to withdraw from the exhausting jobs available to them and give full attention to home and children" (1997, p.215). However, she also highlights the fact that, for young women with few domestic responsibilities, the chance to earn money and to socialise outside the limits of the family sphere can be interpreted in a positive way. Thus, "empowerment" is by no means an automatic outcome of paid employment for all women.

*Changing Forms of Masculinity*

As I stated earlier, most of the gender and development literature and specific gender policies have focused on women as gendered beings and have not really considered the same dimensions for men. This is increasingly changing, however, as researchers are identifying particular problems experienced by men and there is a realisation that the desire to transform or challenge existing gender relations cannot come from women alone (Cornwall, 1997).

In Mexico, as I have highlighted above, men have been working in MNC factories, and in some cases men, particularly sons, will be engaged in some aspects of housework. Gutmann (1996), in his excellent work on a working-class district of Mexico City, stresses the diversity of male roles and identities, highlighting how women's entry into the labour force, foreign influences (especially television and film), and the rise of the feminist movement had all affected gender relations within the community. Despite such evidence of fluidity and change, the domestic division of labour and patriarchal attitudes remain relatively entrenched in many cases throughout Mexico.

There is, however, increasing evidence of projects aimed at challenging these processes (see Chant & Gutmann, 2000). A good example is a non-governmental organisation called *Salud y Género* [Health and Gender], which was formed in 1992 by health workers and whose main activities relate to awareness-raising workshops. The project started off as a women's health project, but the women who attended felt that men ought to be involved as well. This NGO now has single-sex and mixed group workshops. Topics that are particularly focused on with the men are violence, alcoholism, sexuality and parenthood. Following the workshops, participants are expected to return to their institutions and organisations and replicate some of the activities, so that the benefits of the workshops can be spread beyond the limited numbers of attendees (Chant & Gutmann, 2000; EngenderHealth, 2002a).

MEXFAM, the Mexican Foundation for Family Planning, which is affiliated with the International Planned Parenthood Federation [IPPF], has also begun to realise the importance of including men in its programmes. Globally, family planning and reproductive health issues have often been regarded as purely an issue for women, but, while many programmes have had success in the uptake of contraceptive use and improved levels of female health, the exclusion of men from this arena has limited their effectiveness. In some cases, these policies follow a "welfare" approach, as outlined by Moser, within which women are only targeted by development schemes in their roles as mothers and wives. EngenderHealth, an international health NGO with a particular focus on the gender dimensions of health, describes (2002b) the work of MEXFAM and highlights how the approach to men has changed. While MEXFAM offered vasectomy services and the treatment of sexually transmitted infections to men from the 1970s, by the late 1990s it was clear that this work was insufficient and did not really consider the gendered position of men within Mexican society. Following this, MEXFAM organised focus groups of men to develop a video for training purposes. Men identified issues such as violence (against women and between men), excessive alcohol consumption and negotiation between couples. The video is now used in participatory training events, similar to those run by Salud y Género, to help men understand their socially constructed position in society and how they can make changes in their everyday lives.

*Conclusions*

In this paper, I have highlighted the importance of considering the gender dimensions of development. Using Mexico as an example helps us to focus on the impact that economic, political and social processes have on development and the ways in which men and women experience development. I have also stressed that not all men or all women experience policies in the same way, so we need to be wary of assuming female disadvantage in all situations. However, as both national-level statistics and small-scale studies demonstrate, there are structural features in Mexican society that mean that women are generally disadvantaged, relative to men.

Macro-level policies, such as the structural adjustment policies and neo-liberal approaches to development adopted in Mexico since the early 1980s, have had detrimental impacts on vast numbers of Mexicans, both male and female. However, in many cases it is women who have taken on even more of a burden, because of their socially constructed roles as homemakers, as well as contributors to household income. For some women, these policies have opened up opportunities to enter the labour force and, in some way, to gain greater control over their lives, as with Claudia, the tortilla-maker, and some of the factory workers described by Fernández-Kelly. Additionally, middle-class women may be better able to deal with the daily material stresses of economic crisis, because of their financial resources.

At a grassroots level, development policies and programmes can help contribute to the challenging of unequal gender relations, but can also reinforce existing disadvantage. As the discussion of men in development programmes demonstrated, in health programmes men have often been excluded, so leaving household-based inequalities in power and decision-making intact. As this has been increasingly acknowledged, programmes are being implemented to enable these inequalities to be recognised and addressed, so moving towards a vision of "development" that encompasses equity and justice. While these are, as yet, small-scale they do point to an optimistic and hopeful future, building on the recognition that gender roles and relations are not fixed, but are fluid and malleable.

*References*

Allen, T., & Thomas, A. (Eds.) (2000). *Poverty and development into the 21$^{st}$ century.* (Rev. ed.) Oxford: the Open University, in association with Oxford University Press.

Barry, T. (Ed.) (1992). *Mexico: A country guide*. Alburquerque, NM: Inter-Hemispheric Education Resource Center.

Brydon, L., & Chant, S. (1989). *Women in the Third World: Gender issues in rural and urban areas*. Aldershot: Elgar.

Cantanzarite, L., & Strober, M. (1993). The gender recomposition of the *maquiladora* workforce in Ciudad Juárez. *Industrial Relations, 32* (1), 133-147.

Chaney, E. M., & García Castro, M. (Eds.) (1989). *Muchachas no more: Household workers in Latin America and the Caribbean*. Philadelphia: Temple University Press.

Chant, S. (1990). *Women and survival in Mexican cities: Perspectives on gender, labour markets and low-income households*. Manchester: Manchester University Press.

Chant, S. (1994). Women, work and household survival strategies in Mexico, 1982-1992. *Bulletin of Latin American Research, 13* (2), 203-233.

Chant, S., & Gutmann, M. C. (2000). *Mainstreaming men in gender and development: Debates, reflections and experiences*. Oxford: Oxfam.

Chant, S., & McIlwaine, C. (1995). *Women of a lesser cost: Female labour, foreign exchange and Philippine development.* London: Pluto Press.

Cornwall, A. (1997). Men, masculinity and "gender in development". *Gender and Development, 5* (2), 8-13.

Cravey, A. J. (1998). *Women and work in Mexico's maquiladoras.* Lanham, MD: Rowman & Littlefield.

Ehlers, T. B. (1991). Debunking *marianismo*: Economic vulnerability and survival strategies among Guatemalan wives. *Ethnology, 30* (1), 1-12.

Elson, D. (1995). Male bias in the development process: an overview. In D. Elson (Ed.), *Male Bias in the Development Process* (pp. 1-28). (2nd ed.) Manchester: Manchester University Press.

EngenderHealth (2002a). Salud y Género case study: Participatory workshops on masculinity and male involvement. Retrieved August 2002, from www.engenderhealth.org/ia/wwm/emcase4.html

EngenderHealth (2002b). MEXFAM case study: Developing educational materials to promote discussion about male involvement. Retrieved August 2002, from www.engenderhealth.org/ia/wwm/emcase1.html

Escobar Latapí, A., & Roberts, B. (1991). Urban stratification, the middle classes and economic change in Mexico. In M. González de la Rocha & A. Escobar Latapí (Eds.), *Social responses to Mexico's economic crisis of the 1980s* (pp. 91-113). San Diego: University of California, Center for US-Mexican Studies.

Fernández-Kelly, M. P. (1997). *Maquiladoras:* The view from inside. In N. Visvanathan, L. Duggan, L. Nisonoff, & N. Wiegersma (Eds.), *The women, gender and development reader* (pp. 203-215). London: Zed Books.

González de la Rocha, M. (1988). Economic crisis, domestic reorganisation and women's work in Guadalajara, Mexico. *Bulletin of Latin American Research, 7* (2), 207-223.

González de la Rocha, M. (1994). *The resources of poverty: Women and survival in a Mexican city.* Oxford: Blackwell.

Green, D. (1995). *Silent revolution: The rise of market economics in Latin America.* London: Cassell.

Gutmann, M. C. (1996). *The meanings of macho: Being a man in Mexico City.* Berkeley: University of California Press.

Hettne, B. (1995). *Development theory and the three worlds.* (2nd ed.). Harlow: Longman.

Instituto Nacional de Estadística Geografía e Informática (2002). *Mujeres y hombres, 2002*. Aguascalientes: Author.

Jusidman, C., & Eternod, M. (1994). *La participación de la población en la actividad económica en México*. Aguascalientes: INEGI.

Karl, M. (1995). *Women and empowerment: Participation and decision making*. London: Zed Books.

Kopinak, K. (1997). *Desert capitalism: What are the maquiladoras*. Montreal: Black Rose Books.

Lim, L. (1990). Women's work in export factories: The politics of cause. In I. Tinker (Ed.), *Persistent inequalities: Women and world development* (pp. 101-119). New York: Oxford University Press.

Maquila Portal (2002). Maquila overview. Retrieved August 2002 from www.maquilaportal.com/

McClenaghan, S. (1997). Women, work and empowerment: Romanticizing the reality. In E. Dore (Ed.), *Gender politics in Latin America: Debates in theory and practice* (pp. 19-35). New York: Monthly Review Press.

McIlwaine, C., Chant, S., & Lloyd-Evans, S. (2002). Making a living: Employment, livelihoods and the informal sector. In C. McIlwaine & K. Willis (Eds.), *Challenges and change in Middle America: Perspectives on development in Mexico, Central America and the Caribbean* (pp. 110-135). Harlow: Longman.

Momsen, J. H., & Townsend, J. (Eds.) (1987). *Geography of gender in the Third World*. London: Hutchinson Education.

Moser, C. O. N. (1993). *Gender planning and development: Theory, practice and training*. London: Routledge.

Murphy, A. D., & Stepick, A. (1991). *Social inequality in Oaxaca: A history of resistance and change*. Philadelphia: Temple University Press.

Närman, A. (1999). Getting towards the beginning of the end for traditional development aid: major trends in development thinking and its practical application over the last fifty years. In D. Simon & A. Närman (Eds.), *Development as theory and practice: Current perspectives on development and development co-operation* (pp. 149-180). Harlow: Longman.

Pearson, R. (1995). Male bias and women's work in Mexico's border industries. In D. Elson (Ed.), *Male bias in the development process* (pp. 133-163). (2$^{nd}$ ed.) Manchester: Manchester University Press.

Pearson, R. (2000). Rethinking gender matters in development. In T. Allen & A. Thomas (Eds.), *Poverty and development into the 21st century* (pp. 383-402). (Rev ed.) Oxford: the Open University, in association with Oxford University Press.

Potter, R., Binns, T., Elliott, J., & Smith, D. (1999). *Geographies of development.* Harlow: Longman.

Potter, R., & Lloyd-Evans, S. (1998). *The city and the developing world.* Harlow: Longman.

Roddick, J. (1988). *The dance of the millions: Latin America and the debt crisis.* London: Latin America Bureau.

Rowlands, J. (1997). *Questioning empowerment: Working with women in Honduras.* Oxford: Oxfam.

Safa, H. I. (1995). *The myth of the male breadwinner: Women and industrialization in the Caribbean.* Boulder, CO: Westview Press.

Samarasinghe, V. (1997). Counting women's work: The intersection of time and space. In J. P. Jones III, H. J. Nast, & S. M. Roberts (Eds.), *Thresholds in feminist geography: Difference, methodology and representation* (pp. 129-144). Lanham, MD: Rowman & Littlefield.

Selby, H. A., Murphy, A. D., & Lorenzen, S. A. (1990). *The Mexican urban household: Organizing for self-defense.* Austin: University of Texas Press.

Simon, D., & Närman, A. (Eds.) (1999). *Development as theory and practice: Current perspectives on development and development co-operation.* Harlow: Longman.

Stephen, L. (1991). *Zapotec women.* Austin: University of Texas Press.

Stevens, E. (1973). Marianismo: The other face of machismo in Latin America. In A. Pescatello (Ed.), *Female and male in Latin America: Essays* (pp. 89-101). Pittsburgh: University of Pittsburgh Press.

Stewart, F. (1995). *Adjustment and poverty: Options and choices.* London: Routledge.

Tello, C. (1991). Combatting poverty in Mexico. In M. González de la Rocha & A. Escobar Latapí (Eds.), *Social responses to Mexico's economic crisis of the 1980s* (pp. 57-65). San Diego: University of California, Center for US-Mexican Studies.

Thomas, J. J. (1995). *Surviving in the city: The urban informal sector in Latin America.* London: Pluto Press.

Townsend, J. G., Zapata, E., Rowlands, J., Alberti, P., & Mercado, M. (1999). *Women and power: Fighting patriarchies and poverty.* London: Zed Books.

United Nations Development Program (2000). *Human development report, 2000.* New York: Oxford University Press.

United Nations Development Program (2001). *Human development report, 2001.* New York: Oxford University Press.

Willis, K. (1996). Negotiating dualisms: Women, locality and employment opportunities in Oaxaca City, Mexico. *Singapore Journal of Tropical Geography, 17* (2), 195-212.

Willis, K. (2000). *"No es fácil, pero es possible"*: The maintenance of middle class women-headed households in Mexico. *European Review of Latin American and Caribbean Studies, 69,* 65-82.

Wright, M. (1997) Crossing the factory frontier: Gender, place and power in the Mexican *maquiladora. Antipode, 29* (3), 278-302.